WHOSE *Daughter* ARE YOU?

May you be blessed as you discover all that the Lord intended when He created women

Shirley

Shirley L. Diggle

Copyright © 2015 by Shirley L. Diggle

Whose Daughter Are You?
by Shirley L. Diggle

Printed in the United States of America.

ISBN 9781498442213

All rights reserved solely by the author. The author guarantees all contents are original and do not infringe upon the legal rights of any other person or work. No part of this book may be reproduced in any form without the permission of the author. The views expressed in this book are not necessarily those of the publisher.

Unless otherwise indicated, Scripture quotations taken from _the New International Version (NIV). Copyright © 1973, 1978, 1984, 2011 by Biblica, Inc.™. Used by permission. All rights reserved.

Scripture quotations taken from the New American Standard Bible (NASB). Copyright © 1960, 1962, 1963, 1968, 1971, 1972, 1973, 1975, 1977, 1995 by The Lockman Foundation. Used by permission. All rights reserved.

Complete Jewish Bible, David H. Stern, Copyright 1998 by Jewish New Testament Publications, Inc., P.O. Box 615 Clarksville, Maryland 21029 U.S.A.

www.xulonpress.com

Dedication

For my Lord Jesus, who has patiently and lovingly taught me about being a woman. And for my beloved husband Paul. We have walked through many adventures together as Jesus has introduced us to His Father.

Acknowledgements

Though writing a book is a rather solitary exercise, no one ever writes a whole book without the help of many friends and relations. I have been blessed with more than my share of 'helpers' as I've explored this topic of being a 'helper' as Eve was described in the book of Genesis.

Year after year a group of ladies who know each other as "The Sisters" have faithfully gathered and encouraged/pushed me to put down on paper all that the Lord has revealed about being a godly woman. Without their push I doubt that I would have persisted. Most especially I must thank Janet Wilson who has encouraged, inspired and taught me when I wrestled with doubts, mental blocks or weariness. I could never have done this without your help, suggestions and cups of coffee dear Janet Louise. Thank you.

Special thanks must also be expressed to Orith Cunningham who returned to Israel with her husband Willie, a number of years ago. We miss them greatly. Orith graciously agreed to teach my husband Paul and me the complexities and delights of the Hebrew language. We will be forever grateful! Not that we were great students but Orith gave us a window into a whole new world of understanding the Bible and brought colour and light to black letters on white pages. Todah rabah Orith!

I must also thank Bruce and Lorraine Friesen and Jason Goertzen at Lifetree Ministries in Victoria for their encouragement and willingness to make available their facilities every year for us to meet, sing, play, enjoy and fellowship together. I thank you so very much.

There are not enough words in the world to begin to thank my husband Paul for all that he has done to encourage and support me in our more than half a century together. We have climbed mountains together, weathered storms, both physical and spiritual, played and prayed as we've come to know the Lord more. Every Shabbat you honour me and humble me as we break bread and drink wine together and pray for our four children and 12 grandchildren. Thank you seems too small a word!

To my Lord Jesus–Yeshua–I can never thank You enough. You are the best match-maker in the world and I look forward to spending eternity in Your magnificent kingdom. Thank You. Thank You.

Shirley Diggle
Victoria, B.C. Canada
May, 2015

Table of Contents

Introduction xi

1. A Time to be Born 15
2. Ezer: Image Bearer, Theologian, and Warrior 38
3. What Do You Believe and Why Do You Believe It? 56
4. Words Matter 69
5. R + R–R = R & R 81
6. Developing Intimacy 97
7. Called, Equipped and Sent Out 117
8. Becoming God's Friend 123
9. Preparing For A Wedding 133
10. Did I Enlist Or Was I Drafted 150
11. What Is Spiritual Warfare? 166
12. Weapons of Mass CONstruction 185
13. Women Arising 196
14. Lambs, Dogs and the Future Rematch 208

INTRODUCTION

I magine a conversation in heaven between the Father, the Son and the Holy Spirit. They might have been sitting around a table enjoying each other's company and planning the creation of the universe. Being God, this was before time began and before there was any establishment of how long a day might be. And, being God, this was also before Their magnificent creation had been usurped by a fallen angel, who was another of Their own created beings. A bride for the Son was on the top of the list of Their intentions for this new world. She had to be perfect in every way. So They planned for every possible exigency that might spoil or disrupt Their perfect plan. Nothing was left to chance. And it was so!

"The Lord God said, "It is not good for the man to be alone. I will make a helper (an **ezer knegdo**) suitable for him."…….. So the Lord God caused the man to fall into a deep sleep; and while he was sleeping, He took a part of the man's side and closed up the place with flesh. Then the Lord God made a woman from the part he had taken from the man, and he brought her to the man." Gen 2:18, 21-22.

Years go by, hundreds, perhaps even thousands or hundreds of thousands of years and we eavesdrop on another conversation.

"Abraham said to the chief servant in his household......"I want you to swear by the Lord, the God of heaven and the God of earth, that you will not get a wife for my son from the daughters of the Canaanites, among whom I am living, but will go to my country and my own relatives and get a wife for my son Isaac." ......Then he (Eli**ezer**) prayed, "O Lord, God of my master Abraham, give me success today, and show kindness to my master Abraham. "See, I am standing beside this spring, and the daughters of the townspeople are coming out to draw water. May it be that when I say to a girl, 'Please let down your jar that I may have a drink,' and says, 'Drink, and I will water your camels too'; — let her be the one you have chosen for your servant Isaac. By this I will know that you have shown kindness to my master". ...... Then Eli**ezer**, Abraham's servant, asked "Whose daughter are you? Please tell me, is there room in your father's house for us to spend the night?" Gen 24:2-4, 12, 14b, 23. (NASB)

****

Being born is probably the most important event of one's life. It is also the event that we have the least control over. We cannot choose where we will be born–a city, a village, a hospital or a mud hut. We have no choice in the time period we will be born into–war time, peace time, Middle Ages, 20th century, morning or evening. We don't get to pick our parents or our family or whether we will be first born or last. No one ever asks us to choose a name we would like to be called or even if we like the name somebody else has chosen. Perhaps the most defining characteristic of all–we have no choice in our gender.

Introduction

By the time I was 20 years old I was convinced that being female was definitely not an asset. I was quite certain that God had made a dreadful mistake when He created me to be a woman and I frequently told Him so. Many times I asked Him what He could possibly have been thinking when He created Eve. He has never given me a direct answer which is probably a good thing as my attitude really deserved a good spanking or worse, rather than an explanation. However, in His goodness, He has led me along a very long and often lonely path and taught me what an honour He has bestowed on me in making me one of His daughters.

Over the last number of years I have had the privilege of sharing what I have learned with a small group of women who get together every year to share with one another and to learn what it means to be a Daughter of the Lord. We refer to one another as The Sisters. This book is a blending of some those Retreats.

Chapter 1
A Time to be Born

"There is a time for everything, and a season
for every activity under heaven:
A time to be born and a time to die,
A time to plant and a time to uproot,
A time to kill and a time to heal,
A time to tear down and a time to build,
A time to weep and a time to laugh,
A time to mourn and a time to dance,
A time to scatter stones and a time to gather them,
A time to embrace and a time to refrain,
A time to search and a time to give up,
A time to keep and a time to throw away,
A time to tear and a time to mend,
A time to be silent and a time to speak,
A time to love and a time to hate,
A time for war and a time for peace."
Eccl. 3: 1-8

E very person who has ever been born comes equipped with one personalized set of circumstances that includes birth order, economic family conditions and social standing as well as many other uncontrollable things including gender. It is almost like a puzzle or a maze where the objective is to find the best way home without getting totally lost. It is always a challenge. It has been designed that way, both for people and for other creatures. If we try to help a butterfly break out of its chrysalis the poor thing will die because it needs the struggle to strengthen its wings so it is able to fly. Helping a bird to break out of its shell will leave it weak and unable to fend for itself. It is a strange paradox that without struggle there is no strength.

My own journey through the maze of life began in Saskatoon, Saskatchewan during that terrible conflict known as World War II. For over a decade before the war there had been a very serious economic depression that had gripped the whole world, not just Canada. Men travelled from town to town looking for work. Times were very hard. Coupled with the economic situation was a terrible drought that greatly affected the farming communities who depended on crops for their livelihood as well as their food sources. Hope and faith took as big a battering as bank accounts during those years.

The Great Depression had put many plans on hold. Yet, in spite of all that, young people still fell in love, still got married, still had babies. My parents had lived through all those wartime struggles during the first World War, and then the depression strife of the 1930's, but were full of optimism as they planned their future together in 1935. That took a great deal of courage and commitment.

Due to economics and some illness that put my mother, Rachel's nurse's training on hold, they had to wait until December 27, 1937 before they could finally become man and wife. On that day John

Streeter took Rachel Cowley to be his lawfully wedded wife. They planned and dreamed of the day when they could have their own home and family. They wanted a boy and a girl–in that order–to be named David Charles and Shirley Louise.

Alas for plans! World War II interrupted everybody's hopes and dreams. Once again young men and women prepared for war; prepared to leave family, home and country to fight on the other side of the ocean. Two of my father's brothers joined the Royal Canadian Air Force and one of my mother's sisters joined the Canadian Army. Family ties were at once precious and fragile. Life was very hard and fear dominated every conversation.

Suddenly there were jobs available for everybody as industry geared up to provide all the equipment and munitions needed for the War. All those new workers needed housing which was in very short supply. The government initiated a massive building program that saw about one million very modest box-like houses springing up in towns and cities like mushrooms after a heavy rain. Row after row of identical houses, known as wartime houses, lined the new unpaved roads of greatly expanded towns all across the prairies. The house my parents lived in was not that large but there was such a housing shortage that citizens were encouraged to rent out any extra space they had. To help make ends meet my parents took in boarders. Food was rationed also, especially sugar, flour, eggs, meat and butter. My Mother had to become an inventive cook to feed everybody in the household.

Such a time to be born! In July, 1940 the first of the babies my parents dreamed of was born but it wasn't the planned son. It was a little daughter, Shirley Louise, who cried a lot. One of the stories told is that my poor father would put me in a carriage and wheel me along the railway tracks, bouncing over the lumpy ties to try to get me to sleep. Two years later another pregnancy came with the hope that this surely would be their son. It was however, another daughter, Mary Elizabeth, who, for some reason, was always called Betty.

At about that time my father took a job in Moose Jaw, Saskatchewan, in a plant that was building and repairing planes for the war effort. Moose Jaw was very flat and very cold in winter. My mother was so glad that my Dad didn't have to go to fight overseas as her dad had done in WWI. Because he was deaf in one ear he was not able to join one of the military forces. So she endured the cold and the wind of Moose Jaw. Great dust storms blew so much top soil away that sometimes the sky was dark in the middle of the day. I remember the feeling of dust and grit stinging my eyes and face as we walked along the street while I tried to stay hidden behind my Mum's coat.

Many years later Dad admitted that as well as repairing planes he also went up with the pilots to test them to make sure they were airworthy which was actually just as dangerous as being in a battle. It was too late then for Mum to be fearful.

The war finally came to an end and the troops came home. There was no longer a need to repair planes so Dad went back to repairing cars. Life continued to improve economically as well as socially. I was now old enough to go to school and though it was scary to leave my Mum and sister it was also very exciting to be able to learn how to read and to count and to be a "big girl".

It was also during this time that I first went to dancing lessons. After all I was named Shirley with the hope, like millions of other little girls in the country, that I could learn to be like the curly headed moppet who had stolen everybody's affection, the pretty Miss Shirley

Temple. Tap dancing was all the rage at the time so Betty and I learned to shuffle and tap our feet to the music.

Mum also taught both Betty and me to knit during the long winter afternoons. We actually learned to knit on four needles and made socks for ourselves. Mum had to turn the heels for us but we did the rest of the knitting. That would certainly not be considered a beginners project but perhaps she didn't have any other needles or wool available. I loved the making of things.

Then on a very cold day in February 1947, another baby was born. This time the long awaited son, David Charles, filled all their dreams for their family. Shortly after the birth the family moved back to Saskatoon and my parents bought their first home. There was no indoor plumbing; the heating system was an oil burning stove in the middle of the big main room of the house. In the winter exquisite frost pictures decorated all the windows every morning. Close to the heater it was toasty warm but at night we had to wear several layers of clothing to bed because it was so cold.

Baby David's health was not the best and whether it was the cold, or the rather primitive house, it was decided that a more permanent move to the West Coast was going to be both advisable and necessary. During the war all Mum's family had moved from the farm where she had grown up in Saskatchewan to North Vancouver in British Columbia. Following the war Dad's three brothers and their families had also moved there. In the late summer of 1948, after helping Dad's sister and brother-in-law with the harvest, we also moved to North Vancouver. The mountains and the sea were a very new experience for us children but for Mum the relative warmth of the West Coast and the nearness of her extended family were a very welcome change indeed. I missed the huge open skies where you could see for miles.

It was a very new experience to have many cousins, aunts and uncles to visit and play with. Our first Christmas was unforgettable– there was no snow! We walked a few blocks to our grandparents home where 15 relatives, whom I hardly knew, including a great grandmother and a great aunt, gathered for dinner. There were a few extra friends as well. We all crowded around the ping pong table in the basement to do justice to a huge feast that seemed to my little girl eyes to be an enormous crowd around a vast table.

Initially we lived with Aunt Pauline, Mum's sister, who had married my father's brother, Uncle Alex, and their two sons but within a few months my parents were able to buy their own home. It was located on about a third of an acre of land, right next to a little Anglican Church. It was an odd house. It looked like it had started as perhaps two rooms and been added to several times in such a way that to get from the smallest bedroom to the bathroom you had to go through every other room in the house. Dad immediately started a renovation program.

That time was probably the most idyllic time in my young life. There couldn't have been a safer community in which to grow up. The Elementary School was just half a block away; church was right next door; and all the neighbours looked out for one another's kids. So whilst you were always safe you also couldn't get away with mischief either! There was a big park with playing fields very close by and we were free to ride our bikes to a swimming hole in summer with all our friends. We played outside until dark on long summer evenings and in winter stood under the street light looking up into the falling snow and delighting in the sensation of rising slowly into the silent snowflakes.

Every Sunday morning the bell of St Clement's Church woke us up with a sound that echoed around the mountains that surrounded us. My sister Betty and I sang in the Junior Choir at church and later joined the Youth Group. To my great delight I was enrolled in ballet lessons. I was quite happy in a dreamy world of make believe and fairy stories and pretty costumes.

Finances continued to be difficult for my parents. Three growing children and a mortgage were a challenge and Mum spent hours with paper and a pencil trying to make her very tight budget stretch just a little bit further. She took a job, as soon as David was old enough, as a helper in a Pre School nearby. David loved it as he now had lots of kids to play with and didn't need to climb under the fence to run away to find some fun. As soon as David was in school full-time, Mum got a job as a Nurse Aid at the North Vancouver General Hospital working nights only. That meant that while Dad was at work and we were all in school during the day she was able to sleep. At night when she went to work Dad was at home with us.

Our growing family had many growing needs. The original house had only two bedrooms and we needed at least three and preferably four. When David got to be too big to sleep in a crib in Mum and Dad's room he moved to the bedroom I had shared with Betty. I then slept on the couch in the living room. It was certainly not an ideal situation as my 'bed' had to be put away every morning and made up every night. There was also no place for me to put my clothes and 'treasures'. So it was decided to raise the whole house by six feet and dig down three feet to provide a full basement. The digging was done first. Day after day both Mum and Dad spent some time digging a bit more and spreading the soil on the garden area. For weeks and months they dug and took wheelbarrow load after wheelbarrow load out from under the house. It was hard work–especially for Mum who was a very small lady only five feet (and ¼ inch) tall. We were never allowed to forget that ¼ inch!

Then came the task of raising the house. Dad contracted a company to come and use special jacks to carefully lift the house inch by inch and foot by foot. That weekend Dad's three brothers and a few friends came to help build new stairs to get up to the house and new foundations and walls for the new basement. It was a huge undertaking. All the men were used to working together on the farm in earlier years and the women kept everyone fed and the children occupied elsewhere. The men also did all the plumbing and the wiring and later installed a new coal burning furnace to keep the much bigger house warmer than the fireplace had been able to do. We felt blessed indeed.

Before winter that year, 1954, Dad had finished all the outside walls and windows and poured the new concrete floor. He built new stairs to get from the main floor to the new basement and roughed in several new rooms which would become bedrooms and a playroom/recreation room. My Mum and Dad worked very hard. In all of my 14 years to that point I can remember only two holidays, both very brief and both visiting family. They poured all their energies into providing a good home for their family.

The New Year brought the usual bouts of colds and 'flu though Mum tried her best to keep us healthy. In early March I caught an especially bad cold and had to stay home from school for a few days. Just as I seemed to be getting better Mum came down with the cold too. She got very sick indeed with what developed into pneumonia.

A Time to be Born

On March 17 Dad said that I should stay home from school to look after Mum because she was so ill. That afternoon I had to call my grandfather for help because the furnace had gone out and I couldn't relight it. When Grandpa came he was so concerned about Mum that, after talking with Dad on the phone, he called for an ambulance to take her to the hospital. I was very, very afraid.

Dad went to visit her every evening but the reports he brought home were not encouraging. We children were not allowed to go to see her as we were considered too young. We went to school and tried to keep up with homework, meals and dishes. On March 20th several phone calls were made to her sisters who had moved to other cities, to come home as soon as possible. In spite of a terrible snowstorm that made driving dangerous they came immediately. Aunty Pauline, Aunty Phyllis and Aunty Josephine were all nurses who took turns looking after her during that night.

At about 3 o'clock in the morning of March 21st I was wakened by the telephone ringing. I was asleep on the couch and had been dreaming that the ringing noise was somehow causing Mum to die. I woke up feeling great dread and fear. It was the hospital saying that one of Dad's brothers was coming to get him because Mum had taken a serious turn for the worse. I spent the rest of that night alone in the dark, not knowing what was happening but imagining the worst.

The night seemed to go on forever. I prayed terrified prayers begging the Lord to heal my Mum. Nothing I had learned in Sunday School had prepared me to know how to pray for this emergency. There was no way I could go back to sleep and I couldn't waken my sister or brother. I was so very alone with all my fears! At about 7 am somebody brought Aunty Phyllis home so that she could get some sleep. Mum died at about 9 o'clock in the morning. She was 42 years old.

I couldn't believe that God would not answer my desperate prayers. I cried. I screamed. Everyone around me was totally devastated. We children couldn't understand how such a terrible thing could happen. It was the end of childhood, the end of dreams, the end of normal family life. I felt confused, angry and totally without hope. I kept asking why? Why? Why?

The days that followed were filled with confusion, tears and too many people. I don't remember who it was who told me that now I would have to take my mother's place. Somehow we got through the funeral and Betty and I did our best to write thank you notes to all the friends and relatives who had sent flowers and food. In the following weeks we had help from many of Mum's friends who taught us how to do laundry, make pastry and cookies, and to make a grocery list before going shopping with Dad. We learned things young teenagers are not supposed to know how to do. It was impossible to fit in with other girls at school who were going to dances and movies. I was grocery shopping and ironing clothes.

It was not that people were not very willing to help us–they certainly did! They made sure we were fed and clothed. Friends and relatives were extremely generous and caring about our physical needs. But nobody asked about how we were doing emotionally. There was no such thing as grief counselling at that time. We were expected to just pick up our pieces and carry on. Undoubtedly this was a war-time hangover as nobody was deliberately being callous towards us. Each of the four of us lived in our own little bubble of grief.

We continued to waken every Sunday to the bells of St Clement's and we continued to go to church. The Young Peoples Group was a safe place to have some fun and be with other teens. Our minister and his wife were hugely supportive of Betty and me. Unfortunately David, who was so much younger, was badly neglected.

One night we were all talking about what we wanted to be after we graduated from High School. I said I wanted to be a minister but was immediately told by our minister, "You can't". I wanted to know why not. The answer was devastating. "Because Jesus didn't choose any girls." I had already formed an opinion that being a girl was not the greatest thing in the world and this just put the cap on it. Did God not create me female? Did He really not accept females even though He created them that way? How was that possible?

There were not a lot of career possibilities open to women in the late 50's. Nursing was one option, which didn't exactly sound positive to me considering what had happened to my Mum. Teaching, secretarial, office work or marriage were the very few others. The fields of law, medicine, Christian ministry, engineering, forestry and most others were extremely hard or impossible to get into without a fight and I wasn't exactly up for a fight. In my thinking it was another strike against being a woman.

After graduating from High School I tried to make some plans for what I wanted to do with my life. It soon became very obvious that a career as a ballet dancer was now out of the question. I enjoyed learning so I thought I might be able to be a Home Economics teacher. I certainly knew about the 'home' part, and the 'economics', as well I loved the sewing side of that field of study. However it also required a University degree and that cost a lot of money which my Dad certainly could not afford. The only solution was to get a job and save some money to be able to go to university later. It was discouraging to see my friends getting ready to go into nurse's training or teaching that autumn but there was no such opportunity possible for me.

After many days of answering newspaper ads I finally found what I hoped might be a job that could lead to a career. A new modeling agency was looking for a receptionist and I went for an interview. A few days later I got a call offering me the position with the possibility of being trained as a fashion model. I was thrilled. However, within a very few days it became obvious that the director of the 'school/agency' really had other things on his mind. One afternoon he locked me in a room and raped me. I have no idea how I got out of there nor can I remember how I got home that day. I only know I never went back there!

That was the day I put on a mask. I had no one I felt I could trust, no one in whom I could confide, no one I could talk to about such a terrible event. Apart from being a girl what had I done wrong? Just like when my Mum had died I wondered why the sun still shone every day. There was so much shame that I could hardly breathe. It made me want to choke, but I was locked into my own little world where everything was grey. I felt absolutely alone and utterly worthless especially concerning any relationship with a holy God. My hopes and dreams didn't matter because there was no way I could control circumstances. It felt like another death that coloured the lenses that I used to look at life for many, many years. It was years later before I could get out from the terrible secret that got heavier and heavier before I was able to be released from the burden and let in some light.

Looking back from a distance of over 50 years I now believe that what that man was really intending to do was to set up a call girl service and planned to 'train' girls to be prostitutes. As I have remembered things I heard but didn't understand at the time I believe that the modeling agency was just a front for a very nasty business that grossly demeans women.

It was during this time that my Dad met a lady where he worked and decided to marry her. Our family home was sold and we had to move to another part of the city. It was not just a matter of moving house. Even though I could never take my mother's place in my Dad's life, to a great extent I had taken her place in our household. Now that place was being taken by a new woman in Dad's life. Very soon they began to plan another move–this time eventually to California. I felt like I was being abandoned. Hopes and dreams of ever going to university were dead and buried.

Although we look back on the 1950's as a time of stability, the cold war was a daily part of all news reports. My own personal turbulence was very reflective of the unsettled undercurrent of the times. People were building bomb shelters and storing extra food in case of sudden war. I vividly remember the fear following some of the atomic tests that put vast amounts of radiation into the atmosphere. There was a sense of helplessness of being able to do anything to protect oneself from outside forces and decisions made by known and unknown other people but which greatly affected one's own life, choices and decisions. There was an undercurrent of fear and helplessness that made it very difficult to plan any sort of career.

Still, I needed a job if I was ever going to be able to go to university, not to mention support myself. I was able to get a job in a bank in downtown Vancouver. The salary wasn't great, only $135.00 a month, and it was very obvious that, at that time, women did not hold any managerial positions so this would certainly not be a long term career. However, for the time being it was a job. On the first day

I worked there I was introduced to a young man named Malcolm. He invited me out to dinner and seemed very nice. He was a Christian, gentle, polite and very courteous. Perhaps? Perhaps? Could this be a new path for me? Could I possible trust again?

Then I discovered I was pregnant from being raped! I was totally devastated. I had nobody I could call on to help me. Several times I contemplated suicide but decided I was too much of a coward to follow through with it. I began to make plans to go away somewhere and put my baby up for adoption. Keeping the child might have given me a family of my own but I was really aware that I could not earn enough to look after myself much less a baby also. I felt utterly hopeless and totally alone. The shame and fear were overwhelming and I felt desperately afraid of the future.

I felt I could not live at home any longer so I moved into the YWCA. It took almost my entire salary to pay for my room and board. I had less than two dollars left to buy toothpaste and any bus fare I needed. My first plan had been to go to another province to have my baby but I discovered that I would have to prove paternity before an adoption could take place. This I was unable to do. I really needed help so after a few months I confided in the Residence Director at the Y and in the young man I had met at the bank. They helped me to make plans to go to another city in the province where I lived and arranged for transportation and a couple for me to stay with in the new city. I felt terribly ashamed and cried so many, many tears.

The day I signed the adoption papers I was told that after one year the records would be destroyed and there would be no way to ever trace my son. This felt like yet another death. There was no way I could ever reach my mother and now there would be no way to ever connect with my child. I went into deep grief! But it was grief that I could not share with anyone because I had only shared this tragedy with four other people. I had no hope for my future.

I returned to Vancouver and to my room at the Y and resumed my job at the bank. Gradually I picked up the pieces of my life and even found myself smiling occasionally. When the tears would overflow, as they did quite frequently for a start, my friend Malcolm would say to me "Shirley, you can't get clean by wallowing in the mud. You must look up to Jesus!" It took many, many months but after a couple of years I started to think again of going to university. I began by taking some night school courses and daring to hope. I still wanted to be a teacher after all.

On the other hand Malcolm also wanted to go back to university. His long-time ambition had been to go into medicine. I did everything I could to encourage him to pursue that dream, little realizing what an 'earthquake' the Lord had planned for me just around the corner. It had been my dream that he and I would marry some day. Malcolm quit his job at the bank and went for a couple of weeks holiday before starting his studies. It was the last part of August, 1962.

On August 27, a young man walked into the bank and wanted to open an account. Usually I didn't have to look after customers but since it was lunch time it was part of my job to wait on customers. He had just arrived the night before from New Zealand to go to university to do a Forestry degree. Within minutes I had found out a great deal about him; where he was living, his purposes for being in Canada as well as his name and, not to forget, how much (or how little) money he had. I got him settled with an account, a chequebook, a passbook and said "Welcome to Canada".

He returned again the next day. This time it was not lunch time but he asked to speak to me. He said that in order to finish his registration at UBC he needed a doctor's certificate. Since I had been so helpful the day before could I please suggest the name of a doctor. I gave him the name of my own doctor and again said 'goodbye' thinking that that was the end of that.

But he came in again the next day, though I can't remember what his reason was that day. I got the idea that he was lonely since the term had not yet started and there were very few people living in residence at UBC yet. So I invited him to go to church with me on Sunday. At the time it seemed like the right thing to do. When I realized that I would probably have to spend the rest of the day with this man that I didn't know at all I panicked and phoned my pastor's wife. Bless her heart, she invited us to go home with them for lunch after the service on Sunday. Whew!

When Malcolm returned from his holiday I introduced him to Paul since they were both living on the same campus at university. One afternoon they met together and like the gentlemen they both were, agreed to court me and try to win my love. For the next few weeks things got complicated–and very busy. Paul invited me to lunches and dances and Malcolm invited me to concerts and films. There were many dinners and walks as well as going to church. Mercifully, before we all died of exhaustion, Paul asked me to marry him. Before I could answer him I had to take all my courage in my hands and tell him about the son I had given up for adoption. It was the hardest thing I had ever had to do in my life. I risked all his possible rejection and misunderstanding but I couldn't go into a marriage without being very truthful and transparent about such a huge issue.

The next afternoon at work somebody called me and said that a man wanted to speak to me. There was Paul with a huge box of flowers in his arms. Inside were a dozen red roses and a note that said

"The past can stay in the past. I just love you and I want to marry you. Love Paul". My tears were tears of pure joy and I gave him a very affirmative answer to his proposal.

So on March 2, 1963 we were married.

It would be really nice to be able to write "And they lived happily ever after" but this is real life and real life is not like that.

The next years were very busy. Paul really wanted me to be as much at home in the great outdoors as he was. He is an avid hunter, fisherman, and photographer. He took the time to introduce me to a world I knew very little about and I enjoyed every minute. Sometimes he came home with wild orchids in a juice can that had been part of his lunch; sometimes it was pretty pebbles he had found in a stream. He shared what he was learning in his classes about climate, wildlife, and the biology of how forests grow. I learned to identify and recognize trees and the difference between a Mallard duck and a Hooded Merganser. A whole new world opened for me.

In 1965 Paul finished his degree in Forestry and after graduation we prepared to go to New Zealand where he had an obligation to repay the New Zealand Forest Service for their support while he was studying. Many circumstances, that were not always pleasant, brought us to the point of deciding to return to Canada in 1968. We bought a house in Victoria, gave birth to two daughters and a son and became pretty much the same as most other young couples our age.

Though we always continued to go to church, there didn't seem to be much connection between reading the Bible, praying and going to church with the daily problems of paying a mortgage, raising children and balancing a budget. My experiences years before had taught me that God has big plans for men but not for women. He didn't seem to hear my prayers especially when it came to things like plans, dreams and healing. Those old words spoken to me when I was just a teenager followed me around like a dark cloud that never produced refreshing rain. "God didn't choose any women."

Until! Until April 1978 when my concept of who Jesus is received a huge upgrade that I am still working through. We had taken the children to New Zealand for Christmas the previous December and when we got home, I was scheduled to have surgery on my hands to relieve a carpel tunnel condition. Somewhere on the journey home I must have had contact with somebody who had mumps because just a week after returning home and a couple of days before I was to go into hospital I came down with a great case that made me look like a greedy chipmunk. It seemed to be an affliction reserved just for me as none of the rest of the family caught it. Through gritted teeth one dinner time I prayed as the family held hands, "Lord, Your word says that all things work together for good for those who love the Lord, so please show us what good can possibly come from mumps. Amen"

Because of the mumps the surgery was cancelled and just before the rescheduled date Jesus healed my hands through prayer, without the aid of any medication or surgery. Whilst we were delighted, relieved, startled and somewhat bewildered, we were really challenged about who this God is who could just say "Be healed!" and it was done. Our 'Sunday School' Jesus had never mentioned anything about such a thing happening in our time. More importantly, if Jesus could do this what else could He do that we were not expecting or prepared for? Thus began an adventure that has spanned many years, innumerable books, many seminars and conferences and a great deal of soul searching, being stretched and prayer. We will never be the same.

A few days after my unexpected healing I felt I was to phone my old friend Malcolm and his wife, Judy, to tell them what had happened to me. Judy answered the phone and I shared with her the whole story. There was a strange silence at the other end of the phone. I said "Are you still there Judy?" Then it was my turn to be surprised. She said "Shirley, this morning I was reading James 5 where it says that if any among you is sick he should call for the elders and he will be healed. I was telling the Lord that I did not understand that as I don't see that happening in the church today. Then you phoned just a short time later." We were both astounded. It seemed to me to be a confirmation of what had happened to me.

I had heard quite often that 'God has a plan for your life' and in my head I always added, "Sure, but only if you are male! I wish He'd let me in on the secret if that is true!" I can't remember where I heard it or read it but it came as a bit of a shock to learn that Satan also has a plan for your life. How can Satan possibly know any of my plans for my life? Well, I told him. Every time I shared a dream or hope, idea or plan, I was sharing that with more than just my family or friends. The very last thing Satan wants is for Jesus to be able to bring another life into the Kingdom of God so attacking hopes and dreams are a perfect place for him to start to destroy the Lord's plans in a person's life. Reaching your destiny and bringing glory to God is the last thing Satan wants you to be able to do. Often there are generational patterns that are set up that also bring a stop to hopes and dreams. It takes courage to dream and I had learned to not hope lest I be disappointed again.

Jesus had a lot of my thinking to untangle before He could begin to change my attitudes and expectations. Quite early in the process a very dear friend asked me what the Lord called me. She explained that my parents may not have asked what my name should be, the way parents did in the Bible. I had to agree since there were so very many little girls who had been named after Shirley Temple. In one of my elementary school classes there had been four girls named Shirley. So I prayed and asked the Lord what He called me. I felt that He replied "You are Sarah, for you will 'mother many.'" Not that I would be 'the mother' of many but that my purpose would be to 'mother people'. My friend went on to say that the place in your life where you are attacked the most is a good indicator of where the Lord wants most to equip and bless you, the place of your destiny. That made a lot of sense to me. It was not just that I had been raped and had to give a child away in adoption but that, for some reason, it had been difficult for Paul and me to have children when we wanted them. My mother had died when she was too young and her mother had died at an even younger age during the influenza epidemic following the First World War. My mother was only 42 when she died and her mother had been only 26 years old leaving two little girls aged four and seven. Without question 'mothering' was a destiny target in my life that had been successfully attacked many times even in previous generations.

It has taken some time to change long-held misconceptions but thankfully the Lord has supernatural patience and is Lord over time. When my hands were healed we were attending a church that had no understanding of healing so we moved to a different church that was very involved in Charismatic Renewal and quite comfortable with the whole process of healing. We were like very dry sponges that couldn't get enough water. We read approximately a book a week for over two years, attended many seminars and conferences and prayed with anyone who was available.

One of the first things we learned about prayer was that if we listened the Holy Spirit would speak into our minds and give understanding. We were at a Bible study group one evening and were praying for a man who was extremely ill. I felt the Lord 'quicken' a verse from Isaiah to me and when I looked for the verse it was exactly what was needed for the situation. I started to cry though I didn't know why. A short time later we were starting to have dinner one evening and I felt that we were to pray for a young man who had been at our church but had left abruptly after being baptized. The family all stopped what they were doing, joined hands and I prayed a very simple prayer; "Lord we don't know where Len (not his real name) is but You do. So whatever he needs right now, would You please take care of him. Thank You Lord. Amen". About a month later Len reappeared at church and I asked him what he had been doing on a particular evening about 6 pm. He got a very wary look on his face and said, "Why do you ask?" I explained what we had done. He thought for a minute and said, "That would have been about 10 pm in Montreal where I was trying to do a drug deal that went very wrong. Someone shot at me and it hit a stop sign near my head. It brought me to my senses and I started right then to return to Victoria." Whew! Praying for a person was really serious business.

We learned about all the different ways that God speaks through dreams, visions, words, impressions, and dark speech. I have always been a very 'visual' person and have a pretty active imagination. Paul, on the other hand, tends to receive impressions and words. For me, when I pray, it is like watching a television screen but without the sound. For Paul, he gets the sound without the pictures. Sometimes we even agree with each other about what the pictures and words actually mean!

We started to attend Friday evening services at an Anglican Church here in Victoria that was very involved in Charismatic Renewal and had speakers come from different parts of the world. Charismatic Renewal was a new church experience for us and a very challenging one in so many ways. It also explained some of the things that were happening to us in our prayer times. One Friday evening we were listening to a lady, Leanne Payne, from the United States who was teaching about the healing of memories. The church was packed and the only place for us to sit was right at the front in the choir stalls. After some background teaching for quite a while, Leanne began to lead people in a prayer for healing as a whole group, through life, beginning with conception and going year by year. The early teen years were hard to get through as I remembered the terrible night my Mum had died. I began to cry as I re-lived that long, lonely, terrifying night. I knew without a doubt that Leanne would also inevitably get to age 18 and I would have to again remember that day that I had tried so hard to forget. I again saw myself in that room. I saw the blue dress that I had been wearing. But before I could 'see' the event again a strange thing happened. Very gently a soft white covering like swans down was tenderly 'placed' in the Spirit, over me from my head to my toes and a quiet voice assured me that "though your sins are as scarlet they shall be whiter than snow". My tears continued but I was no longer quite so embarrassed about being in full view of the congregation. The shame was being washed away. I hardly dared to move and I have no idea what else Leanne taught about that evening. It didn't matter because I was 'caught up' in a sweet place where healing of my heart was beginning. I wanted to just stay there forever. Later I realized that I was not the only person crying that evening. The healing of memories, whether in a group or individually is a very powerful experience.

That was just the beginning of a process that has continued for many years now as the Lord has brought me to a place where I can rejoice in being a woman and delight to share with other women what I have learned.

Chapter 2

EZER: IMAGE BEARER, THEOLOGIAN AND WARRIOR

The Holy Spirit is really an amazing teacher. In 2005 Paul and I went on a tour of Israel with a couple that we had known for quite a few years and about 20 other people who all quickly became friends. After we got home I was sharing one day with some of the women from that group about something the Lord had revealed to me about how He thought of women. After some discussion we all decided to go away for a weekend and I would share more of what I had been learning. What a strange set-up, sharing for a whole weekend about being a woman when I had never wanted to be female.

It seems that wrong attitudes about women are very ancient. The great Greek philosophers hated women and believed they were created by Zeus, the king of the Olympian gods, to punish and afflict men. According to Zeus women came from one of ten sources: a long-haired sow, an evil fox, a dog, the dust of the earth, the sea, a stumbling obstinate donkey, a weasel, a delicate long-maned mare, a monkey or a bee. Women were 'defective accidents' since they were unable to produce the 'seeds' that fathers produced. The thinking was that women were just the soil for growing the seeds that were all presumed to be miniature males. This thinking does not give a lot of confidence for the much renowned Greek logic when clearly both male and female children are brought forth from women!

The Romans were not a lot better. Roman women were mere possessions with no rights at all. Roman men had three names–a clan name, a family name and a personal name. Roman women got only a clan name and a family name but then a feminine form of their father's name. So Gaius Julius Caesar's daughter was Julia. Marcus Tullius Cicero's daughter was Tullia. If there was more than one daughter it was Julia elder (or younger) or Martia secunda or Tullia tertia etc. The Romans were allowed to kill deformed or unwanted babies except for boys and the first born girl. They legislated keeping at least one female alive. Roman burial records show twice as many adult male burials as females. Female deaths were not even worth recording.

Think about how radically different the Judeo/Christian thinking is concerning women. Woman was 'fashioned' not created, to be a helpmate, companion and equal, to bring God's kingdom on earth as it is in heaven. The original Hebrew language uses the words 'ezer knegdo'–the word ezer when by itself, is applied to only four persons in scripture: God the Father, God the Son, God the Holy Spirit and Eve. Hebrew is a very descriptive picture language where every individual letter has its own meaning. The picture painted by the words 'ezer knegdo' is of a river, the river of life, enclosed between two banks. The banks of a river are very often different. One bank could be forested, or a field of grass, or even a rocky cliff. The other bank could be where a family grew barley or pastured sheep. Unless both banks do their job the river will not run properly. If either bank fails to do its part there will just be a swamp.

Though not quite as outlandish as the Greek or Roman thinking, nonetheless the Judeo/Christian attitudes towards women have also been crippling for both women and men. For a very long time the mistaken interpretation of 'helpmate' has been 'helper' as in carpenters helper, gofer, or servant. God did not plan for women to be just somebody to do the man's cooking, or cleaning. Think for a minute what conditions were like in the Garden of Eden. They were both naked so what laundry was there to do? All their food grew right where they were so there was no grocery shopping to do. There were no children yet so what childcare was needed? Children didn't appear until after the Fall. Houses had not been invented so there was no house cleaning to do. What was the woman to 'help' the man to do? It was not her great physical strength that was needed. God had said that it was not good for the man to be alone and then He caused all the creatures of the earth to pass before Adam so that he would know that there was not another creature that could be a suitable helpmate for him. Adam had to <u>know</u> that he needed Eve. In Matt 6:8 Jesus said "Your Father knows what you need before you ask Him" so before Adam even knew that he had a need, God already knew what He planned to do for His ultimate creation. It is very clear that Eve was to be much more than just a companion designed to relieve loneliness.

Adam and Eve were created in God's image. The mandate they received from God was to "Be fruitful and multiply, and fill the earth, and subdue it; and to rule over the fish of the sea and over the birds of the sky, and over every living thing that moves upon the earth." However, God did not give a lot of details about roles, job descriptions or division of responsibilities–at least not that were recorded.

He did not give them any suggestions as to exactly how He expected them to carry out those orders. Surely God knew that the possibilities for messing up were/are endless.

Without giving this very much deep thought I have always assumed that 'being fruitful and multiplying' meant having children and we have surely accomplished that–now about seven billion of us! However I am now realizing how sloppy my thinking has been and I am having to revise my previous interpretations somewhat. Let me explain.

When God created Adam and Eve and put them in the Garden there was already war happening in the heavenlies. We don't know precisely at what point Lucifer rebelled against God and was expelled from His presence but we do know that at some point Lucifer was renamed Satan and was banished to earth. He desired to be higher than God, to set up his throne above God's throne and that started a war in heaven. When he was defeated and thrown out, he took one third of the angels with him. Sadly that was not the end of the war but there was a change of venue. Satan was banished to earth and continued his fight from here as it says in Isa 14:12-21. Verse 13 says "But you said in your heart "I will ascend to heaven; I will raise my throne above the stars of God. And I will sit on the mount of assembly in the recesses of the north. I will ascend above the heights of the clouds; I will make myself like the Most High." The passage prophesies the downfall of Satan and also his end!

In creating Adam and Eve God was not creating a mere romance in a beautiful garden, with the final chapter to take place in another wonderful garden at the end of time. No, the first couple were actually recruits in the terrible war that has been raging on the planet from the very beginning. If we unpack the Hebrew meaning further we learn that the words 'ezer knegdo' infers "to identify the enemy" and to plan for his downfall. Though He didn't spell it out exactly in scripture in all the fullness that most of us would like to have, God gave Eve four tasks; to identify the enemy, to identify his tactics, to plan a strategy to defeat those tactics and then to work with Adam to bring that defeat about.

Let me ask you a question: "Is Satan your enemy?" The answer should be "no". He is actually God's enemy and we are the prize. The reason Satan hates us so much is because we have been created "in the image of God." In the very first conversation he had with Eve, Satan deceived her with a lie. He suggested that if she ate the forbidden fruit she would "be like God". She already **was** like God. She was created in His image as was Adam. It is for that very reason–the image that we bear–that Satan hates us with an unholy passion. We bear an image that inherits eternal life through the redemption that Jesus achieved on the cross. There is no redemption for fallen angels.

Many years ago Paul and I were challenged with the question: What did Jesus get from the crucifixion? Putting it a little differently– what did we get? Obviously we got everlasting life, forgiveness of sins, fellowship with God both now and after we die. But for Jesus, what was His reward? He didn't need a collection of sins. He has never asked one of the angels to bring Him the sin collection for March 26, 2010 or any other date. He already has everlasting life. What He won for the Father is a holy people for a holy God. In fact He won for Himself a bride to reign with Him for all eternity. He defeated Satan at the cross and since then we have been fighting a battle with a predetermined victory.

We need to look closer at some of the implications of being "in His image". If you go into any Post Office in this country you will see on the wall a photograph of Queen Elizabeth. It is her image that represents her authority in Canada. Her image is also on stamps, coins and other currency and thereby declares the legitimacy of those items. An image of the monarch has power and commands respect. In ancient times, when a king wanted to visit a part of his realm he would send a painting or sculpture of himself ahead of him so that the people would know what he looked like and could greet him appropriately. His image would be on their coins just as today and indicated his authority in the marketplace. He had statues of his likeness erected in various cities in his realm to make himself known–which is how we know what some of these ancient kings looked like.

In downtown Victoria (the city I live in, which is the capital of the Province of British Columbia), there is a statue of Queen Victoria on the grounds of the Legislature. It gets covered with dirt, grime, as well as the leftovers from pigeons, sea gulls and the like. If somebody important is coming to visit, the statue gets a good cleaning because her image represents the name of this city and its heritage.

When we sin we get covered with dirt, grime and sundry demonic droppings and we also need a good cleaning. So when we go to the Lord with a sincere, repentant heart and ask for forgiveness He will never say 'no' because we carry His image! This gives an added understanding to the songs about being 'washed in the blood of the Lamb' or 'Oh the blood of Jesus, it washes white as snow.' In Lev 11:44 God says through Moses "Consecrate yourselves therefore, and be holy for I am holy". That does not mean that we are to try our best to be holy, give it our concentrated effort to be holy as I have always thought. I have struggled with commands like that one and thought "God You know I can't be holy or perfect. You know that I will fail." However, if I am created in His image–and I am–then because I am in His image I CAN be holy through the power of the Holy Spirit living in me. It's not my effort but His image that makes it possible. Holiness means being set apart, consecrated to the purposes of God as His holy people, His holy city as well. We have confused holiness with righteousness, which is being clean before God.

When I was writing this section I experienced an uncomfortable object lesson. My computer got thoroughly messed up and I couldn't access any of my writing or emails or my homepage. Nothing looked familiar no matter how many buttons I pushed. Eventually I called in some tech help. In the mean time I was like a bear with a sore head. I was upset, frustrated, angry–and according to my dear Paul, I was not pleasant company to say the least. One morning I suddenly realized that I was not representing the 'image of God' very well. My bad temper and frustration were doing Satan's work and covering the 'image' with droppings that needed to be washed off. I had never realized before that my reactions–anger, frustration, impatience, judgement and all the other negatives that I struggle with, are part of Satan's plan to spoil God's creation. Eve was deceived about being created in God's image but Satan has also tricked me into not realizing that my negativity was also soiling God's image. I have a new appreciation of Jesus' words in Mark 12:34: "You are not far from the kingdom of God." By my actions and responses I can choose to be conformed to this world or I can walk in the kingdom of God. My actions reveal where I am living.

The call to bear God's image is an amazing invitation to know God on a much deeper, more personal level. Such an invitation implies that His door is always open to us and He desires to include us in the work of building His kingdom here on earth. In other words women, in their role as 'ezers', are called to be theologians but not the kind of theology that comes from many books and much theoretical study. In its simplest terms theology means "the study of God". For most of us that word carries a lot of baggage with it but really all it means is that we are invited to walk with God, to align ourselves with His purposes, to make known His ways to those around us, to share His heart, imitate His ways and love what He loves. It is a call to see every situation from God's point of view and ask for His wisdom.

Think back to the first time the Lord asked you to see something from His point of view. I will never forget when that happened to me. Though I don't remember the exact date I vividly remember where I was and what I was doing. I was part of a Home Group and we were to study the fifth chapter of Romans for the next week. While I was vacuuming I was thinking about Jesus being the second Adam and I said to the Lord "How can Jesus be the second Adam? Jesus brought life and Adam brought nothing but trouble and death. It was because of him that we got kicked out of the garden." (I realize that my language was not very theological.) The Lord replied to me "No he didn't." "Yes he did Lord." "No" said the Lord. "You'd better go back and read it more carefully." So I did. I discovered that it was God Himself who sent Adam and Eve out of the garden to protect them from eating of the fruit of the other tree in the garden–the tree of everlasting life. Having eaten of the forbidden fruit, if they then partook of the fruit of the tree of everlasting life there would have been no possibility for redemption for God's most beloved creatures. That forbidden fruit was actually poison to them. God had not said that <u>He</u> would kill them if they ate of it but that they would surely die–because it was filled with Satan's poison.(Matt 7:20). I have since come to understand that the good side of that "tree of the knowledge of good and evil" is just as poisonous as the evil side. We have all heard the old saying "The road to hell is paved with good intentions" and it surely is! Paul wrote in Romans 7:24 "What a wretched man I am! Who will rescue me from this body of death? Thanks be to God–through Jesus Christ our Lord". I was just amazed. I asked "What else have I got the wrong way around?" The Lord then pointed out that the forty years of wandering around in the wilderness that the Jews regard as punishment was actually training time–sort of boot camp–to go from being a collection of slaves and hangers-on who needed to be told what to do at every turn into a nation who would take orders from the Spirit of the Living God and go into the Promised Land. Though I didn't realize it then I had just had my first theology lesson. I was learning how to see things from His point of view.

All people are image bearers but only women are ezers. Perhaps one of the most important tasks of an ezer is to be that theologian–knowing God's ways and sharing them with men. By the way–that is called submission. You submit or give to another, the understanding the Lord has given to you for a given situation. Submission is part of being a complementary partner. I want to look at a few examples of women in the Bible to illustrate this point. Some of these women you will recognize but others you may not know so well.

Hagar, Sarah's Egyptian slave, had a most interesting experience. Being a slave was the least enviable position in life. She had no rights, not even to her own body. We actually know very little about her and it is not recorded where she went after she and Ishmael were sent away when the lad was a teenager. Much earlier she had a profoundly life-changing meeting with God. In her most desperate time–when she knew that she was pregnant and had been abused by Sarah and sent away, the Angel of the Lord met with her. Even more amazing

He called her by her name. Nobody else ever called her by name. Can you imagine what that did for her? Furthermore the Angel told her that she would give birth to a son and his name would be Ishmael, meaning God hears, and that both she and the child would survive and fulfil the destiny the Lord God had for them both. The Angel then sent her back to face Sarah–perhaps the hardest thing of all for her to do. Her theology was not well developed at this point but Hagar did two things. First she acknowledged that God is different from all the tribal gods and idols she had ever experienced before. Then she gave God a name! She is the only person in scripture–male or female–to give God a name. She called Him El Ro'i–the God who sees me. She might be a nameless slave in Abraham's household but to God she is a person with a name. Second she took her budding theology and lived in the hardest place of all–back with Sarah who mistreated her. Her brief encounter with the Angel of the Lord gave her the courage to make probably the first free choice of her life. Her new understanding of El Ro'i–the God who sees me–was an understanding that Abraham and especially Sarah needed from her. Hagar submitted her new understanding of who God is and made God personal in everyday life.

Tamar was a very interesting and misunderstood lady who started life as a prostitute in Jericho. She attracted the eye of Judah's oldest son Er who married Tamar but because he was a wicked man, the Bible says God caused him to die. Now the custom of that day was that the next son was to marry his brother's widow and provide children for his brother. But Onan, the second son, was also considered to be wicked in the eyes of the Lord so he also died without producing the child Tamar wanted. Judah had a third son, Shelah, who was too young to marry Tamar so Judah sent her back to live in her father's house until Shelah was old enough to marry. Time went by. In fact quite a bit of time went by and Judah's own wife also died. It became pretty obvious to Tamar that Judah had no intention of allowing his only remaining son to produce the child she so desperately wanted. It would seem that Judah must have been thinking that there was something wrong with Tamar rather than with his boys. So Tamar took things into her own hands. She dressed herself up as a prostitute and enticed Judah when he was on his way to shear his sheep. She took his staff and belt as tokens of payment that he would pay her later. She got pregnant as a result. Judah was furious and ordered her to be killed..... until she brought out his own staff and belt and declared them to belong to the father of her child. Judah was caught! His declaration was, "She is more righteous than I".

This story is about so much more than wanting a baby. The Bible doesn't throw around the term 'righteous' casually. Tamar was fighting for a godly principle. For a man to die childless would mean that his line would die out in the nation. This was a matter of national survival–an issue the Jews have faced time and time again over their long history. Judah had only three sons and two of them were dead. So Tamar knew that, though both her husbands had been wicked men, they still needed to be honoured in the line of Judah. So she turned a 'trick' with Judah. Perhaps the Lord had the last laugh because she gave birth to twin boys, Perez and Zerah–two dead sons of Judah–two grandsons to replace their fathers.

However there is another element to this story. It involves the laws of inheritance. Judah's estate would have been divided four ways with Er getting two of the fourths as the first born son. When he died childless Onan now stood to get two thirds of the estate. But if he produced a son for his brother he would be back to the quarter he expected before. So greed entered his heart. Shelah stood to get the whole lot if he did not produce children for his dead brothers. God had a better plan to bring about through a woman who understood the righteous ways of Yehovah. Tamar's first born was Perez who became one of the ancestors of Jesus' line. As well Judah's life was turned around and he became a much better man for Tamar's influence and interference. Though Judah was the head of the tribe he honoured Tamar and accepted her righteous rebuke. It was very much a turning point for Judah in his relationship with the God of his fathers. Judah went on to rescue his brother Benjamin when the brothers went down to Egypt to get grain during the famine. His own grief over the deaths of his sons made him very compassionate towards the grief Jacob felt over the presumed death of Joseph.

As we continue to look at the theology of biblical women, the next one on our list is Abigail, who is described in 1 Sam 25:3 as "a beautiful woman, intelligent and of good understanding". Here is another woman married to a wicked man. Nabal was very wealthy with large herds of sheep and goats. David had a bit of a protection racket going around the Carmel area, southwest of Jerusalem and had kept Nabal's servants and flocks safe during the summer season. When it came time to shear the sheep in late winter David sent his men to ask for provisions as payment for the service David had rendered to Nabal. Nabal refused. So David ordered his men to get ready for battle. When Abigail heard from the servants about David's faithful service and Nabal's refusal she immediately took action. She prepared many needed foods, several jugs of wine and saddled donkeys to ride to David's camp. As she met David and his men on the way she said to him, "Please let your maidservant speak to you, and listen to the words of your maidservant." (1Sam 25:24 NASB) She then went on to prophesy that David would become king over Israel, (he had already been anointed by Samuel), that he would defeat his enemies but that he must not shed blood unrighteously but allow the Lord God to deal vengeance for him. David's response in verse 32 is marvellous. "Blessed be the Lord God of Israel, who sent you this day to meet me and blessed be your discernment, and blessed be you, who have kept me this day from bloodshed and avenging myself by my own hand." Less than two weeks later Nabal died of a heart attack and David sent for Abigail to become his wife. There is no suggestion that David loved Abigail but rather that he recognized that he needed her wisdom (her theology) for his future. By stopping David that day Abigail changed the history of Israel by preventing Israel's greatest king from wilful sin. This is practical theology and the gift of the prophetic at its best.

The last lady we will look at is Mary (Miriam) of Bethany. The first time we meet Mary, her sister Martha was preparing a big meal for Jesus and His disciples. Martha was very annoyed that Mary was not in the kitchen helping her with all the cooking. Instead Mary was sitting at the Lord's feet listening to all He had to say. At no time did Jesus ever rebuke her for wanting to know more about Him and His teaching. Neither did He fault Martha for desiring to serve Him with her best. Jesus loved both sisters and considered them His friends and would never have tried to set up a rivalry between them. In a very gentle way Jesus tried to tell Martha that He would be pleased to have her sitting with Him also. Jesus opened the way even more for women to become theologians and disciples which is their rightful place as ezers. What we need to see clearly about Mary was that in the process of sitting at His feet, she learned to listen to His heart and hear–really hear–His words. Mary, more than any of His other friends and disciples, clearly understood who Jesus was <u>from God's point of view.</u> She understood that He was to be the atoning sacrifice, that He was going to die at the hands of evil men, and that He would rise again. It was not just that she had seen Him resurrect her brother Lazarus. That was a miracle that could only have been accomplished by the Messiah. Lazarus had been dead four days, one day longer than the time period that the scholars of that time taught was the limit of time that the soul would linger before going to sheol.

A few days later Lazarus was among the guests at a banquet given by Simon. In spite of the stares of the men at the dinner at Simon the leper's house, Mary took the most expensive treasure she had, an alabaster jar of expensive perfume, and anointed Jesus for burial. The monetary value of the gift was immaterial. There was simply no other way for her to express her love, devotion, worship and passion for the Man who she recognized as the Messiah of Israel. Think about what she did. In a roomful of men she let down her hair–something a devout Jewish woman simply would not do. She poured out her heart extravagantly in spite of being misunderstood by every man there except Jesus. She had heard the heart of God and so prepared Jesus for the ordeal He was about to endure. The perfume of her sacrifice would have lingered on His body even while He was dying on the cross. What a comfort it must have been for Jesus to know that Mary understood His very human need at that moment. He knew what was coming. Jesus was wholly man as well as wholly God and He needed that human comfort. In that moment He chose to allow Mary to be His ezer. Every one of us have had times in our lives when we needed someone to come and just give us a hug without any words. Just a simple hug. Mary's action assured Jesus that at least one person believed the deeper story that His very life had been telling for over three years. It was not until after the resurrection and ascension that the disciples finally got it.

The third part of being an ezer (after image bearer and theologian) involves being a warrior. I said earlier that the three times that the word ezer is used in the prophets it is always in the context of military action. In the 16 times that ezer refers to God it always indicates powerful military language. God is described as deliverer, helper, shield of His people and a powerful sword. In the psalms He is described as more dependable than chariots and horses. In fact the verb form 'azer', which means to rescue or save, occurs approximately 80 times in the Old Testament and generally indicates military assistance. But for some reason when the word ezer refers to women the translators change the meaning to restrict it to making babies, cleaning house and being submissive to a man.

All of us are familiar with Proverbs 31–the ideal wife. Our English translations don't do justice to the Hebrew words. In Hebrew if you didn't know that this was supposed to be describing a woman you would think it was talking about a military hero. In verse 15 the Hebrew says she "arises like a lioness while it is still night, and provides prey for her household." Verse 17 says she "girds her loins with strength and her arms are strong for their tasks." In English verse 29 says "many daughters have done nobly but you excel them all" but the Hebrew portrays her "going out to battle". In English verse 25 says "strength and dignity are her clothing and she smiles at the future" but the Hebrew says "she laughs in victory".

If there was any doubt about the need for women to go to battle consider the fact that in the New Testament book of Ephesians the armour that Paul talks about is not restricted to men only. There is no suggestion that women are not included in putting on the whole armour of God and standing firm to be able to resist the assaults of the devil. Female armour does not come with pink frills. We are meant to be equipped, battle-ready warriors able to report for active duty.

There are times when it is helpful to look at what is happening 'in the world' to know what God is doing next. Usually Satan tries to precipitate and contaminate God's plans. For example: In the last couple of decades or so there was a huge feminist movement that swept the world. Some of the antics, such as burning bras and mass demonstrations to enable public nursing of babies were a bit silly. However, the rational behind much of the turmoil was quite justified because there were injustices that were not only tolerated but were also considered 'normal'. Different wage levels for the same work, different laws for parental rights, different standards for divorce, inheritance or education opportunities were obvious grievances. In some countries there are still severe inequalities in education, medical care and land and business rights. As with so many things that Satan tries to influence there were extremes. Now we are confronted with political correctness, nominal quotas of women in politics and the work place and, worst of all, feminist theology–God is female. Truly Satan tries to make God's job harder and too often we co-operate with the wrong theology.

It is becoming obvious that the Lord is calling women to take the place He planned for them at the very beginning of creation. We were never designed to compete with men but rather to complete the fighting force that the Lord needed. Some time ago we heard a most interesting observation in a radio interview about the killing of reporters in Iran. The Iranian woman being interviewed was a TV and newspaper reporter and though she was not a Christian, what she had to say is something we need to hear. As a reporter in Iran she was followed for months and every day her home was watched by no fewer than 16 people. She was a wife and the mother of three young children. She and her husband noticed that between midnight and 6 am there were no watchers on guard. They arranged to go to visit family in Montreal for a holiday–a perfectly normal thing to do. One night, after the watchers had gone home, they bundled their three children into the car, took a few possessions in suitcases and went to the airport. Originally they thought they would be home in a few weeks or months but it has now been over six years and they cannot go back home. The thing that she said that is so important for us to hear is this: The women of Iran are rising up TOGETHER to force change in the government. The authorities cannot intimidate them because they stick together and will not knuckle under in fear. Division is one of Satan's oldest tricks along with fear, isolation and conformity. At this time in Iran those tactics are not working. The women are rising up against the Islamic efforts to keep women 'in their place'. These women are ezers and they are warriors.

Radical feminism tried to make men our enemy but in reality we are supposed to fight WITH men against God's enemy. We have been deceived into thinking that men are our enemy. From God's point of view the sons of Adam and the daughters of Eve are supposed to be a Blessed Alliance bringing the kingdom of God on earth as it is in heaven. As ezers we are image bearers, theologians, warriors and partners in the Blessed Alliance. We don't become ezers when we marry, or when we have children and then suddenly stop when we are widowed or our kids grow up or we never marry at all. Our task as ezers is not dependant on marital status or age. We are ezers as little girls and as old women.

When Jesus was speaking to the Samaritan woman by the well in John 4:23,24 He told her "that true worshippers shall worship the Father in spirit and in truth; for such people the Father seeks to be His worshippers. God is spirit and those who worship Him must worship in spirit and in truth". I believe that in Genesis when God said to fill the earth and subdue it that He was referring to the war that was already happening (we need to subdue it) and that filling the earth meant to learn how to worship Him and to inspire others to also worship Him. We are created in His image which makes such an undertaking possible. We are invited to know Him intimately which makes being a theologian extremely desirable. We are equipped to be warriors with fellow soldiers both male and female as companions. We are called to be a great company of women–ezers–who hear the Lord give the command to proclaim the good tidings that will cause the enemy to flee as it declares in Psalm 68. It is time to rise up.

Chapter 3

WHAT DO YOU BELIEVE AND WHY DO YOU BELIEVE IT?

I attended a seminar one autumn that was led by a man from Ontario. Something that he said made me quite upset and started me on an intensive study of my Bible. He claimed that "the blood is just a symbol–the cross is the most important thing." Our Bible is a very bloody book. There is blood on almost every page and our God wants us to know why. Because if we don't know WHAT we believe and WHY we believe it, we can be persuaded by any fast talker to believe almost anything. In this chapter I want to clarify some of 'the what and the why' of our Christian faith.

Our God initiated a sacrificial system right at the very beginning. According to 1 Peter 1:14-20 it was before the foundation of the world–before anything had ever gone wrong–the sacrificial system was already an essential component of God's plan. When man was created in the image of God, the freedom to choose to obey, to honour and worship the Lord God, was a privilege given to no other creature. Not to birds, not to fish, not to any other animal was given the possibility to feely choose close relationship with the Almighty. That ability to choose also brought the option of choosing to sin. The thought that His special people would possibly sin was so abhorrent to Father God that only the precious blood of His beloved Son was deemed sufficient to cover such a terrible calamity. When the Father, Son and Holy Spirit were discussing how They were going to create this world They determined that blood sacrifice would be necessary to cover the possibility of sin. In essence, blood is the most important and precious commodity in the entire universe; there is no life without blood.

We don't know how long it took for Adam and Eve to sin against their creator but when it happened God covered their sin by using animal skins to cover their nakedness. (Gen3:21 God covers the sin of Adam and Eve.) In other words some animals had to be killed, thereby shedding blood, to cover sin. It is interesting to ponder what I would have done if I had been in Eve's place that day when I heard God reveal the result of my sin. I think my first inclination would have been to decide that passing on this curse to children was out of the question. However God said that she would be eager for her husband meaning that avoiding having children was not an option. When her first son was born she gave credit to God for enabling her to bring forth a man.

Initially two sons were born–Cain and Abel. It is obvious from the story in Gen 4: 1-12 that Adam and Eve tried to teach them that they were to bring appropriate offerings to God. Cain brought vegetables and the work of his own hands. Abel on the other hand, brought a lamb from his flock–a blood sacrifice. God accepted Abel's sacrifice but not the work of Cain's own hands and in a fit of jealousy Cain murdered his brother. It is almost like Cain was thinking, "You want blood God?–here, have some of Abel's since You like his sacrifice so much". But God heard Abel's blood crying out from the ground. The first human blood spilled was heard in heaven by God's ears. We have a tendency to muddle in our minds the difference between 'kill' and 'murder'. Both result in death and both spill blood but it is the intent and purpose that makes a difference. The sixth commandment says "Thou shalt not murder" **not** "thou shalt not kill". God does not give to people the right to decide who should live and who should die.

Hundreds of years go by. Mankind has multiplied and largely lost contact with our creator God. So God went in search of a man who would listen to Him and in a very pagan society, in what is modern-day Iraq, He found Abraham and began to reveal Himself. He told Abraham to leave everything he had ever known, his family, his culture, even the gods he had worshipped and go west to a land that he did not know. He made many mistakes along the way, including lying about his relationship with Sarah and using a concubine to produce a son who was named Ishmael–meaning 'God hears'. After a long time of learning to trust God for a son and heir from his own wife Sarah, the couple is blessed with a special son, Isaac, a name that means laughter.

There comes a day when God told Abraham to take his son, Isaac the son of promise, and to go to a place that he will be shown to sacrifice his precious son. We are told that the place was Mount Moriah which is now known as the Temple Mount in Jerusalem. The Lord stopped Abraham's hand from bringing down the knife and caused him to turn and see a ram caught by its horns in a thicket. This ram became the substitutionary sacrifice in Isaac's place. Abraham passed God's test and was willing to trust God with the most precious relationship he had ever had and God counted that act to him as righteousness.

In 2007 during a trip to Jerusalem we stood on the roof of a church and looked towards the Temple Mount. Our tour leader said; "When the ram was caught in the thicket it was as if there was a crown of thorns around his head" and our Jewish guide was visibly moved.

In following the history of the Jewish people, more centuries go by and Abraham's descendents became slaves in Egypt. God prepared a man by the name of Moses to bring His people out of slavery and into the promised land. Through a series of miracles God accomplished two things. In Exodus 12:12 God says, "On that same night I will pass through Egypt and strike down every firstborn–both men and animals–and I will bring judgement on all the gods of Egypt. I am the Lord." God proved that the Egyptian gods were powerless. Then He displayed His own power to the Hebrew slaves in the final contest against the gods of Egypt. The blood of lambs, which was spread on the doorposts and lintels of the houses caused the angel of death to pass over the homes of the Hebrews and kept their firstborn children safe. God gave them very specific instructions for how to prepare for the journey they were about to take and what to ask their Egyptian neighbours for as plunder. Then they were to eat the roasted lamb in haste with their cloaks on. They were to take the sacrifice right into themselves and eat it to give them strength for their journey. In the same way we take within ourselves the elements of communion to strengthen ourselves also for the journey we are on. (Ex 12: 7-13)

During their journey through the wilderness the Lord gave the people two more major pieces of His ultimate plan–the Tabernacle with all its furniture and sacrificial system, and the Ten Commandments. Many chapters of the Bible are given over to very detailed instructions for the Tabernacle; of how things were to be made, what different kinds of offerings were to be given, who was to carry and set up the tabernacle and many more details. We will look at only two things. The "scapegoat" was an animal that was to have laid on it all the sins of the people and then be led out of the camp to wander and die in the wilderness. Someone else must carry our sins away. For us that 'someone' is Jesus. Secondly, each family was to bring an animal to be sacrificed. The father of the family was to catch the blood in a basin as the animal was killed so that the realization of the cost of sin became very real to all the family members. Sin cost a life and the life is in the blood. It is the father–even our Father God–who has the responsibility of making that truth real to each of us. THE LIFE IS IN THE BLOOD. Just as Abel brought a lamb from his flock, and the Israelites were told in Egypt to kill a lamb, the lamb is the special animal that sacrificially was most used to cover sin in Old Testament times.

The second piece of God's ultimate plan of redemption, the Ten Commandments, have not been well understood by westerners I'm afraid. They are commandments–not ten suggestions–and to our individualistic ways of thinking seem old fashioned at best. All those "thou shalt nots"….. don't seem very relevant in our relativistic society. The first five commandments concern our relationship with Father God and the second five govern our relationships with our fellow man. Too many times we hear people say things like "I don't steal and I haven't killed anybody so they really don't relate to me." But if you turn the commandments from negatives to positives the picture changes considerably. 'Do not steal' becomes 'give generously'. 'Do not murder' becomes 'bring life'. 'Do not bear false witness' becomes 'live the truth and handle it with care.' 'Do not commit adultery' becomes 'honour, respect and esteem relationships with the opposite sex at all times'. 'Do not covet' becomes 'when you live according to God's law you will be content'. The law is meant to keep us from harm and ensure life and prosperity for us. It is not so much that we keep the law but that the law keeps us.

In Isa 53:1-12 Isaiah prophesies that the Messiah is 'the lamb of God' upon whom would be laid the iniquities of us all. Earlier, in Isa 7:14 it says that a virgin would give birth to a son and his name would be called Immanuel which means "God is with us". In Micah 5:2 it says that Bethlehem would be the birthplace of Messiah. We are all so familiar with this story that most of us don't ask all those pesky 'why' questions. Why Bethlehem? And why a virgin? And why during that particular time period?

One question at a time. Why Bethlehem? The name of that town means 'house of bread' and Jesus said in John 6:25 "I am the bread of life". It is most logical for the 'bread of life' to come from the 'house of bread'. Jesus was also called "the lamb of God who takes away the sin of the world". Bethlehem was the place where lambs that were used for sacrifice in the Temple in Jerusalem were raised. Bethlehem is just five miles south of Jerusalem. Where you find flocks of sheep you would expect to find shepherds and Jesus identified Himself as the Good Shepherd.

There are a few other questions we must ask about Bethlehem also. If Bethlehem was Joseph's 'hometown'–and a census specified by Caesar Augustus directed each man to return to his hometown– why were there no relatives who could take the young couple in? Why were they forced to find a stable? Was it just that there was no room at the inn or had the stigma of illegitimacy closed many doors and hearts to Mary and Joseph? On the other hand is not a stable a suitable place for a lamb to be born, even the Lamb of God? As well

Bethlehem was the hometown of Israel's greatest king, King David who was also a shepherd in his early years. In 2 Sam 7: 16 the Lord makes an amazing promise to David. He declared "Your house and your kingdom will endure forever before Me, your throne will be established forever." The genealogies at the beginning of Matthew's and Luke's gospels are there to prove that both Joseph and Mary are from the line of David and thus give legitimacy to Jesus' right to the title of "Son of David" and inheritor of David's throne.

Next question–why a virgin? The answer to this becomes very fascinating. Jesus was fully God and fully man. The angel Gabriel told Mary that the Holy Spirit would come upon her and she would conceive in her womb and bring forth a son. In other words God would be the father of the child. This was dramatically confirmed at the beginning of Jesus' ministry when the voice from heaven declared at the Jordan River, when Jesus was just beginning His ministry, that "this is My beloved Son. Listen to Him". Mk 9:7 That was a divine verification of the fact that Jesus is the Son of God. Though we don't know for sure how old Mary was, it is thought that she was probably in her early teens, perhaps 14 or 15 years old. From her Jesus received His humanity but from the Holy Spirit He received His God nature. We are also assured that Mary was a pure virgin about as uncontaminated as it is possible for a human being to be. Thanks to science we now know that during pregnancy the blood supply of the mother and babe NEVER co-mingle. Nourishment and waste products pass through a membrane but the baby's blood is wholly contained within himself. So Jesus' blood could truthfully be said to be sinless since it never co-mingled with His mother's. Thus His blood is a pure, sinless offering to cover the sins of the world.

One other question needs to be considered at this point. Why did Joseph not leave Mary in Nazareth when he knew that she was so close to giving birth? Could it have been that he feared that the people of Nazareth might stone her while he was gone? Was Joseph's concern for her safety what the Holy Spirit used to make sure that Jesus was born in Bethlehem and so fulfil prophecy? What does this possibility do to fill in the picture we have of Joseph who, in so many ways, is a very shadowy figure and not well appreciated?

The time period is also most interesting. There was never a time before and has never been a time since when there was relative peace in that area of the world, with a common currency, a common language, good roads, few barriers between nations and the mighty Pax Romana, the Peace of Rome, to enable easy travel and exchange of ideas. It seems incredible but within a few years knowledge of Jesus and the Christian faith had spread to millions of people from Great Britain to India and beyond–without the aid of the internet, radio or TV!

During Jesus' life Satan tried many ways to kill this Man who was destined to die. The first time was when King Herod slaughtered all the baby boys in Bethlehem who were two years old or less after the Wise Men had visited the king to inquire about the birth of a new king. Herod was an extremely violent, jealous man who deliberately eliminated any person he viewed as a rival including people within his own family. Then during the temptation in the wilderness Satan again tried but failed to work his tricks to deceive Jesus as he had managed to deceive Adam and Eve. He tried again in Nazareth when the people tried to throw Jesus off a cliff. A storm on the Galilee in the middle of the night with His disciples in a fishing boat that was in danger of being swamped was Satan's next effort. Jesus, however, was not going to just die. His blood had to be shed in a particular place, at a particular time for a particular reason.

Then on a fateful day that had been planned and prepared for from before the foundation of the world, Jesus was crucified in Jerusalem, on Mount Moriah of old–the very same place that Abraham had taken Isaac centuries before. There had been prophetic words, promises, covenants, religious feasts all pointing to this culmination that would fulfil what had been planned for so long. The sign over Jesus' cross condemned Him in three languages–Greek, the language of culture, Latin, the language of government, and Hebrew, the language of religion. (John 19:20) At the very time that the Passover lambs were being killed in the Temple, just a short distance from His cross, Jesus' blood was also being shed for the sins of all mankind. That cross, that pointed upward to heaven and outward to all mankind, was the instrument the Father chose to use for the shedding of Jesus' precious blood but it was the blood that brought redemption to us, not the cross. Death came into the world from the tree of the knowledge of good and evil but the 'tree' that was Jesus' cross brought redemption and life.

The cross is important for sure. It has two sides–the side of death but also the side of resurrection. Jesus didn't stay dead. Praise God! Jesus laid His life down–it was not taken from Him. In John 10: 17-18, Jesus said, "The reason My Father loves Me is that I lay down My life–only to take it up again. No one takes it from Me, but I lay it down of My own accord. I have authority to lay it down and I have authority to take it up again. This command I received from My Father." Now Jesus is alive forever more. What is more, when we put our faith in Jesus we are called to live on the resurrection side of the cross. Because the life is in His blood.

Let's go back for a moment to Genesis 2:7. When God created Adam He took some of the dust of the earth and formed a man. That man was perfectly shaped with all his parts in exactly the right places. He had arms, legs, hair, eyes, lungs, everything. But until God blew into his nostrils and filled those lungs with air, Adam's heart was not pumping blood through his body to make him alive. Blood is the only thing in our bodies that travels to every part of us and touches every single cell bringing nourishment and eliminating wastes. Only blood brings life to our bodies because the life is in the blood.

An illustration of this dynamic principle is found in the story of the valley of dry bones in Ezek 37: 9-10. The bones and sinews and other parts all came together but until the breath of the wind came from the four corners of the earth–that is the overwhelming breath of the Holy Spirit, the Ruach Ha Kodesh–there is no life in those bodies. Like God blowing His breath into Adam's nostrils, God started their hearts beating and the blood flowing bringing energizing life. The breath and the flowing blood caused them to stand up ready to fight, full of life, a great army that brings victory.

Sometimes we get so familiar with what we read in our Bibles that we no longer see the meaning. All of us have read, and sung and talked about the body of Christ. Jesus is the head of the church, we are all parts of one body, we are saved by the blood of the Lamb, and so many more very familiar words. Let's stop for a moment and take another look. If we are the body of Messiah then where and what is the blood that will cause us to be alive since the life is in the blood? Is it the Holy Spirit who feeds and nurtures us together as a body? In that case the blood of Jesus does a great deal more than just cleanse us of our sins. Our own blood takes nourishment to every cell in our bodies as well as eliminating wastes so it stands to reason that the blood of the body of Jesus will have to do no less. The waste products in the church are obvious–sin of every sort, quarrels, jealousy, rage, factions and much more. But what are the nourishments of the church? In John 10:10 Jesus said "I came that they might have life and have it to the full." Think about Jesus' words in John 6: 53-58, "I tell you the truth, unless you eat the flesh of the Son of Man and drink His blood, you have no life in you." For most of us that sounds very gruesome. The communion service that commemorates the instructions Jesus gave at the Last Supper in the upper room in Jerusalem are detailed so tenderly in John chapters 14–17. The Apostles Creed talks about the 'communion of saints' which is very close relationship with one another, in fact, knowing one another's needs without being told about them. There is comfort and security in a close community of fellow believers that both keeps us from harm and ensures assistance when it is needed, that in our 21st century cities has virtually disappeared. We need to resurrect that loving support system.

I had a very interesting experience a number of years ago regarding the 'communion of saints'. For several days I was struggling with a serious health issue. Out of the blue I had a phone call from a friend who said that the lord had told her that I was in need of prayer and she wondered what was going on. I was surprised but shared with her what was happening. She said she would pray. The next morning another friend called about the same time of day with the same message. The two ladies did not know each other so I knew it had to be the Lord. A few hours later a third friend called with the same story. The next morning an Anglican minister from another town called and said that the Lord had told him that I had a need for some prayer. By this time I was feeling that the Lord was not just alerting friends to pray but was perhaps blabbing about my need. Each friend told me the same thing–the Lord wanted me to go to bed and rest. So I did. There are many other things that we are called to do by the Holy Spirit to build up the Body of Christ–prayer, Bible reading, worship and others. Hebrews 10:6 declares "a body You have prepared for me." God doesn't do this TO us but He has chosen to do it THROUGH us.

Recently when I was talking with my friend Janet, she mentioned that in Revelation 12:11 it talks about "they overcame by the blood of the Lamb and the word of their testimony". This is a verse we quote fairly frequently but I'm not sure we really know what it means. As I've come to appreciate that the 'blood of the Lamb' is so much more than just a covering for our sins I wonder if it is really the glue that will hold us together through whatever trials are coming. Is this what held the early Christians together? When we read in the first chapter of Revelation about overcoming do we have any idea just how we can do those things? As our society yearns for fellowship, is the blood of Messiah the missing ingredient that causes us to fail or at least flounder in our efforts to evangelize and build community? Can we have a valid testimony, I wonder, without being totally immersed in the blood of the Lamb? Is it more than My testimony–is it more a case of OUR testimony that will be the overcoming factor? I think we've really got a lot more to learn about overcoming as well as about the power of the blood.

Francis Frangipane wrote in a book called "This Day We Fight"; "There is an enemy at our gates. Though you may not be aware of Satan's assaults, are you praying with authority against him? If not it is probably because Satan's first line of attack is often a spirit of heaviness, which renders Christians passive and thus defenceless against the unfolding battle. Indeed if you aren't praying against the enemy he is probably stealing something precious from you–and it may be the heart of a loved one, the future of your church or the destiny of our nation".

Our God is calling women all over the world to rise up. Every day in the media we hear of women in India, China, Iran, as well as North America, rising out of situations of subservience and apathy and refusing to endure degrading situations any longer. In Psalm 68 it says that the Lord will give the command and great will be the company of women who will rise up to be a great host that will defeat the army coming against His people. That includes us. We will need to be united heart and mind. We will need to know each other as daughters, sisters and women who can work together, laugh and cry together and be united in love for one another and yearn for our coming Bridegroom with passion, intelligence and single heartedness.

It is reported that at one time Alexander the Great said; "I am not afraid of an army of lions led by a sheep: I am afraid of an army of sheep led by a lion". This is a tremendously exciting time to be a woman. Our God, who is known as the Lion of Judah, is calling.

Chapter 4

WORDS MATTER

Our God is very faithful! If you are willing to listen He is more than willing to speak to you. He is also very persistent. As I was researching for this topic of how God sees women I asked Him if He had something more He wanted to tell me. It was like opening a floodgate. The Lord showed me so many ways that He is raising up women all over the world. I got emails, magazine articles, television stories, books, books and more books, and most of all, the Lord's assurance that He is preparing His women for a very new adventure with Him. We are coming into a very exciting time to be a woman. God really loves women.

You know it wasn't that long ago that women in Canada were declared to be "persons". I'm not sure what we were before but on October 18, 1929, the Privy Council of Great Britain ruled that "the Governor General of Canada shall summon qualified persons to the Senate and the word persons includes members of the male and female sex." In Canada complete Federal enfranchisement for women was in effect by 1918. The first province to grant women the right to vote was Manitoba in 1916 but Quebec not until 1940!

When I graduated from high School in 1958 I started to work in a bank. At that time a single woman, no matter her age or occupation, was not eligible to take out a loan or mortgage in her own name alone but had to have her father, grandfather, brother, uncle or son co-sign for her. She was also not permitted to sign for herself to have a surgical procedure in a hospital. It was quite rare to have a female doctor and even more rare to have a woman lawyer. We have come a long way in less than 60 years!

Looking back gives us an interesting perspective on what is happening today. If we see only what has occurred in the last 10 or 15 years we will miss the bigger picture of God's intentions for women and the relative speed of change that is occurring. Quite apart from anything else we can also have considerable appreciation for the struggle of the Native peoples, African Americans and other minority peoples who have had to fight to be accepted as intelligent, legitimate people who can be valued citizens.

I don't intend to get bogged down in the so-called battle of the sexes. Every one of us has been affected by that war. War between the sexes was never part of God's plans for His precious sons and daughters. There have been enough books written, magazines and films concentrating on the problem so we don't need to add to the stack. I will just share one fine example that really seems to sum it all up. In a book entitled "Clementine Churchill" and written by her daughter Mary Soames (pub by Cassell, London England) it records a letter written in London, England by the remarkable Lady Clementine Churchill, March 30, 1912.

She wrote to the Editor of The Times responding to a very pompous, 3000 word essay from an eminent physician, Sir Almoth Wright who was objecting strenuously to the granting of the vote to women on psychological and physiological grounds. Lady Churchill wrote:

Sir,

> After reading Sir Almoth Wright's able and weighty exposition of women as he knows them the question seems no longer to be 'Should women have votes?' but 'Ought women not to be abolished altogether?' I have been so much impressed by Sir Almoth Wright's disquisition ...that I have come to the conclusion that women must be put a stop to. We learn from him that in their youth they are unbalanced, that from time to time they suffer from unreasonableness and hypersensitiveness. Later on in life they are subject to grave and long-continued mental dis- orders, and, if not quite insane, many of them have to be shut up. Now this being so, how much happier and better would the world not be if only it could be purged of women? Is the case really hopeless? Cannot science give us some assurance, or at least some ground of hope, that we are on the eve of the greatest discovery of all–i.e. how to maintain a race of males by purely scientific means? And may we not look to Sir Almoth Wright to crown his many achievements by delivering mankind from the parasitic, demented and immoral species which has infested the world for so long?
>
> Yours obediently,
> C.S.C. ('One of the doomed')

Our Father God has a very different plan for women that we haven't really seen yet. The words of Psalm 68 give us a little glimpse into what He is beginning to shape in our day. I wish there was a timeline that was delineated but perhaps it is just as well we don't know that yet.

For many years I have asked the Lord what He intended when He fashioned Eve from Adam's rib? What did He have in mind when He created Eve? I was hugely encouraged when I learned about the 'ezer knegdo'–the Hebrew words in Genesis 3:18 that are translated in our English Bibles as 'helper' or 'helpmeet'. Unfortunately it conjures an image of a carpenter's helper or a 'go-for'. In Hebrew it means so much more than just somebody to do the cleaning, cooking, picking up Adam's socks and bearing children. Hebrew is a very 'picture' language and these words picture the two banks of a river that are both very necessary to function in the purpose of defining, guiding and establishing the river of life. If either bank fails to function, all you have is a swamp. Genesis states very plainly that men <u>and</u> women were created equal but with different functions. Somehow that concept has been horrendously twisted over the millennia and so we have the battle of the sexes.

During one of the recent wars in Gaza, an Israeli intercessor wrote about being able to see the 'war beneath the war' using the analogy of a great storm at sea. The waves are huge, the winds roar, the rain pours down in such a storm and it is a terrifying place to be. However, a few meters below the surface of the waves the storm is just background noise and all is relatively calm. In fact scientists have discovered that what is really happening is that all kinds of nutrients are being stirred up to bring new life and vibrancy to the creatures who live in the ocean. In a similar way we need to look at the spiritual 'war beneath the war' that we are called to fight for God's kingdom on earth.

What happens to us when we go through storms? Don't we cower and quiver in the face of things we don't understand or expect? Our initial response is usually fear and an urgent request (that we call prayer) for God to change, prevent, protect, help, help, help! But in fact, God is stirring things up–shaking us–in order to bring new growth.

A number of years ago I had an interesting experience with this lesson about storms we don't understand. We had arranged to take our children to New Zealand for Christmas to visit Paul's parents. Just before we left I was diagnosed with carpel tunnel syndrome in both my hands and surgery was scheduled two weeks after we were due to return on January 31. On February 10 I woke up in the morning with my face badly swollen, barely able to swallow and gritting my teeth to talk. I had mumps! Surgery was cancelled. For two weeks I was in a lot of pain and very concerned for my family that they should not come down with the same ailment. (They didn't.) One night at dinner–which for me was only liquids sipped through a straw–I prayed through clenched teeth "Lord, Your word promises that all things work together for good so please show us what possible good can come from mumps. Amen." The surgery was rescheduled about six weeks later by which time it was early spring. We went to church the Sunday before I was due to go into hospital and I asked for prayer because I was scared. The thought of my hands being cut was very distressing to me. One of the deacons said he would pray for me and if anything happened to delay the surgery, to just trust that God would heal me. That afternoon we worked outside and I was doing things with my hands that I had not been able to do for some time. That night I slept through without waking due to pain from numb, tingling fingers and in the morning I could straighten my fingers and even bend them backwards. When I called my doctor he said that he could not see any reason to go ahead with the surgery so we cancelled it!

We rejoiced but we were also extremely challenged. We knew nothing of a God who could just reach out and heal a person in these days. Surely that happened only in the Bible. Who was this God anyway and what else did we not know about Him? That experience sent us on a quest that continues to this day. We have experienced much new growth from all that was stirred up but quite frankly I think the storm is still raging!

If we look at the 'war beneath the war' in the battle of the sexes we begin to see a rather different picture begin to emerge. There is, and always has been, a spiritual war ever since the Garden of Eden. I want to go back to that time for a few minutes as the Lord has shown me a few things that I missed before.

Sometimes we can get too familiar with a story so that we no longer see all the details. Too often I have thought that God levelled a lot of curses in that story. In fact God cursed only Satan and also told Adam that because of his disobedience the <u>ground</u> was cursed and it would, in the future, be reluctant to yield the crops needed for food. Adam would have to work very hard. But Adam and Eve themselves were not cursed.

We need to think about what God did NOT say. He did NOT tell them they were obviously not a good match for each other and that He would try to find them more compatible mates. There was to be no divorce in the Garden. Nor did He say that Adam would now make all the decisions and Eve was to just do as she was told. Eve's purpose as an equal partner remained as she had originally been designed. I personally believe that when God said that Eve's desire would be for her husband, God was reading her thoughts; that her remorse was so great that she would never want to have children and so pass on to a new generation the horror of her sin. Barrenness was not God's intention for them either.

When God had told Adam that they were not to eat of that forbidden fruit He said "for in the day that you eat from it you shall surely die". (Gen 2:17) God did not say that He would be the one to kill them. We are to understand that the fruit of the tree of the knowledge of good and evil is poisonous to us–both the good side of that tree and the evil side. It is not hard to understand that the evil side of the tree is poisonous to us but we are very prone to compromise with what we think is good. Only close fellowship with the God who loves us can keep us from such compromising.

No, everything God told them was very positive even though at that moment they did not understand. In fact He declared to both of them their destinies and His plans for redemption. He told Adam that he was to be a farmer and that it would be very hard work. God was very honest and didn't paint a rosy picture. Eve was told she would be a stay-at-home mum and a wife to Adam.

How many of us have been told that God has a plan for our lives and we've said, "well I'd really appreciate it if He would let me in on the secret." It is actually quite simple to see that in a community many activities and occupations need to happen but the most important plan for each of us is to find God in the midst of all the busyness of life. We were made for relationship with our God, within families and in larger communities and it is in that context that we find our destinies.

God made it very plain to Adam and Eve that they could not stay in the Garden. Remember there were two trees in the Garden–the tree of the knowledge of good and evil (that was the forbidden fruit that they had eaten) and the tree of life. When you read Gen 3: 22-24 you must hear the anguish in God's voice as He pronounced the consequence of their disobedience and sin. God put into place His most trusted cherubim to guard the path back into the Garden so that His precious human children would not be able to eat of the tree of life and live forever in sin. It was for their own safety that they must be prevented from eating of the tree of everlasting life and thus be condemned to an eternity of separation from our loving God. He revealed to them His plan for a blood sacrificial system for redemption from sin. God Himself killed animals and used their skins to make clothing for Adam and Eve. They were not just told about God's plan but received a personal demonstration that made a huge impact on them. However imperfectly they understood they passed the information on and it has come down even to our own time. Adam and Eve were 'covered' physically with skins and spiritually with blood sacrifice BEFORE God sent them out of His Garden and into this dangerous world.

Fast forward thousands of years to a little town of Nazareth in Israel. It is time for the Lord to bring about the next major step in His plan for redemption from sin.

This is another story that we are too familiar with to appreciate all the background. When Archangel Gabriel told Mary that she had been chosen by God to give birth to the Son of the Most High, Mary had some very legitimate questions. Sometimes the Bible is most frustrating in what it does not say. I like to have a lot more details in stories. Did Gabriel reassure Mary that Joseph would be informed of this change in their plans? Did the angel give her any suggestions of how she could break this exciting news to her parents? No. Gabriel just told her that a distant relative was now six months pregnant and 'nothing is impossible for God'. What a strange thing to say.

Have you ever wondered how Mary got to Elizabeth's home? Reading from the 'gospel according to Shirley' version, Mary checked the Israeli Egged Bus schedule between Nazareth and Ein Kerem, a distance of about 120 miles and toddles off to visit with cousins Elizabeth and Zechariah for awhile. When she arrived she found that Elizabeth had been in seclusion for five months and Zechariah was unable to speak. It seemed that he too had had a visit from Gabriel but he was unable to share with Elizabeth any of the details. Why didn't Zechariah just write down for his wife what the angel said? Was she unable to read? Did he have to do a variation of charades to get her to understand? Or was it that when Mary arrived she actually brought a great deal more understanding and information to both Elizabeth and Zechariah? As the two women talked and prayed together, did the Holy Spirit knit their hearts such that they could appreciate the immensity of what God was doing through each of them and understand their parts in the plan for the redemption of the world? In the ordinariness of their lives God was revealing the destinies of Elizabeth and Zechariah, Mary and Joseph, and the two little boys who would be born. With a little new insight go back and reread the first chapter of Luke again and marvel at what God did through people He chose for His purposes.

In the ordinariness of our lives we also have a part to play in establishing God's kingdom here on earth. The war begun in Eden has yet to be finished. At the moment bombs and bullets are flying in many parts of the world but lies, lust and unbelief are destroying just as many lives here in Canada. In the same way that Mary and Elizabeth were women who needed each other to be able to co-operate with God's plans 2000 years ago we also need one another to become a capable army of God.

We really do need each other! Our culture teaches us to be very independent and isolated from one another especially regarding our struggles, hurts and needs. We could learn much from our Native Peoples in this matter. A number of years ago a tragic fire on a nearby Reserve killed three generations of women in one family. Other members of the family were seriously hurt trying to rescue them. Though the coroners, fire officials and police were all anxious to do their jobs, the Native community wanted first of all to grieve, to properly bury their dead and to mourn for the lost lives. Spiritual and emotional needs came first. They cried together, then they set about to rebuild their lives together. They know how to need each other.

What has happened to our understanding of community? The beginnings of our country were hugely influenced by a pioneering spirit that enabled people to work together for the good of the whole community. As a very young girl I remember going to my aunt and uncle's farm to help with the harvest. The women cooked; the kids did dishes and served tables. Farmers and their wives and children from several farms all got together to help one another. When everybody's harvest was complete they celebrated, danced and sang, often in the schoolhouse or the church which were the centres where people gathered to celebrate, to grieve and to support one another.

What kind of disaster is it going to take to bring people to the point of caring for one another in our day? When are we going to know each other so well that we don't even need to ask for help? In the previous chapter such caring for one another is called the

'Communion of Saints'. To win this ugly war we are going to need to really embrace and practise this much neglected gift of the Holy Spirit.

It is pretty easy to enjoy fellowship when things are going well but when things don't go well—when we are ill, hurt, disappointed, disillusioned, discouraged, ashamed, rebellious, or dealing with any other of Satan's dividing schemes we tend to pull back, to move away from each other. That is when we need each other the most! It is the very time we need to encourage each other. We need to ask the Lord who it is that He wants to strengthen through us this day. Then follow through with a call, an email or a visit.

A few years ago I read about a very wise teacher who knew the value of words. She was having a tough day with her rather rambunctious class and finally had had enough of the teasing and unkind words. She told each student to take out a piece of paper and put their own name on the top of the sheet. Then to pass the paper to the person behind and to write something nice about the person whose name was on the top. Then pass the paper again until every body had written something nice about every member of the class. She then collected the sheets and took them home. The next morning she handed the papers back to the original owners and told them not to tell anyone what was written but just to quietly put them away. There was a completely different atmosphere in the room that continued for the rest of the year. Many years passed. Then one of the students, now grown up and trained as a soldier, was killed in action. One of the things that was found in his wallet was that special piece of paper. It had obviously meant a great deal to him. At his funeral his former classmates brought out their own much folded sheets of paper also and shared with their former teacher how very much those words had influenced them all as they grew up. One person had had the paper framed to hang on the wall. Another had secured it inside the Remembrance book of his wedding. The value of those words had changed their lives.

Our Lord is calling His women to be a great host who will be able and equipped to rise up when He calls. Psalm 68:11-13 says: *The Lord gives the command; the women who proclaim the good tidings are a great host. Kings of armies flee, they flee, and she who remains at home will divide the spoil! When you lie down among the sheepfolds, you are like the wings of a dove covered with silver, and its pinions with glistening gold"*.(NASB) We must learn to develop as a communion of saints so that we will be able to respond to Him quickly when He calls. Our words do truly matter!

Chapter 5
R + R–R = R & R

Like most people we did not get an instruction book with each child that was born to us and at many points we have found ourselves much in need of help when things went wrong. There was a time when we went to see our pastor, Bruce Friesen, for some advice. He gave us a very strange 'formula' which in spite of my love of mathematics, just would not 'balance'. In fact until he explained it, it made no sense at all. "R + R–R = R & R! Rules plus Regulations minus Relationship equals Resentment and Rebellion." Once we understood it we could see that it made a lot of sense. The more we discussed it the more implications we could see for a great many situations beyond our immediate family needs.

When our children were growing up, Paul's job as a professional forester meant that he had to be away from home quite a lot. In order to keep things running fairly smoothly and dependably we had quite a few 'rules'. Every family does. We were a little obsessed with 'doing things right' and we were very involved with church which we also discerned as being about lots of rules and regulations and 'doing things right'. When Paul came home from work or a field trip there were dozens of things that had to be done and he was concerned about doing everything really well. He was, in fact, something of a 'controller'. Okay, more than something! Consequently he didn't develop good relationships with the kids as he was often too tired, too busy or too overloaded with his job. Nor did the kids develop good relationships with their dad. They learned, as I had, quickly to avoid being the object of his impatience.

Over the years the Lord tried several times to get through to Paul that things were not as they should be but without success. It is amazing and very disconcerting how we can be so focussed on our own way that we don't hear the Lord's kind voice. Let me give you an example of the Lord's kind voice. We had a lovely Jersey cow named Muffin for several years who gave us the most wonderful milk and cream. She was also a great deal of constant work. One winter when there was snow on the ground and it was very cold with a bitter wind that didn't stop for days, we had her in a pen where there was also a young steer. Muffin was due to deliver a new calf and the steer was being a big bully and hurt her very badly. It took several days but after much suffering both Muffin and the new calf died. Paul prayed and prayed that the Lord would warm the temperatures, melt the snow, stop the terrible winds, and save the cow that we were all very fond of. Paul prayed everything he could think of. In tears he had to realize that he could not change or control the weather or anything else. So our dear Muffin died.

Still Paul did not see how much he tried to control other parts of his life. So if we won't hear from the gentle messenger God will send a harder one. On December 18, 1990 Paul had a serious car accident in the middle of a blizzard here in Victoria. Paul has never liked the snow and from that day to this he has liked it even less! We rarely get blizzards in Victoria but that one caused many cars and buses to go off the road as well as much damage to property. There were even some livestock losses due to power failures during that storm. Our younger daughter, Heather, was with Paul when they were hit head-on only about a mile from home. The car was a total write off. Heather was bruised and some whiplash but the extent of Paul's injuries was not really clear for several months. He sustained a head injury that took away his career as a forester and put him in a very limited position. He described that time as like being frozen inside a block of ice with little holes to the outside that very muted sound came through but he was trapped inside unable to respond very much. For nearly four years his predominant emotion was anger. He rarely spoke during that time. Often he just sat with his eyes closed though he was not sleeping. It was very hard on the whole family. Being in a room with more than three or four people was more than he could handle which was difficult as we were a family of five. The kids drew away from their dad even more. The two girls were of an age to leave home, which they did–one to get married and the other to live with an alcoholic, drug-addicted boy friend. By the grace of God Paul doesn't remember much about that time but unfortunately the kids still do! The gulf between them only got wider.

Many times during that period I questioned God "why"? Why was it so hard? Why did nothing ever seem to work out for me? When would it ever be my turn to have some kind of success in life? I thought we were keeping the rules so why were we not having the abundant life the scriptures promised? Have you ever been caught in the "why" cage?

The doctors were not much help during that time either. It is very hard to diagnose a brain injury. In an effort to do 'something' doctors treated him with antidepressants that were basically "shots in the dark". In fact it took over seven years until, by God's grace, we were referred to a head injury specialist who immediately recognized the issue as damage to Paul's cerebellum. A broken leg can be put into a cast but not a broken brain. An infection gets some pills and rest along with cups of tea stirred with appropriate amounts of sympathy and in a couple of weeks all is well again. But a brain injury is not like that. It looked like Paul, even sounded like him if he spoke but the real Paul was missing. He had to go onto a disability pension and finances were very tight. Peter was still in High School and, very predictably, got into lots of trouble. I had to try to balance the needs of the kids, Paul's care needs and my own sanity needs. There were times when Paul felt completely lost if we took a different route to get to a store or doctor's office. It would take him days to get re-oriented. Throughout all this time I had to keep a dependable routine which included our daily prayer and Bible reading. That was a constant that kept Paul grounded and the two of us connected when little else did.

It took some time–years in fact–but eventually I realized that the 'abundant life' promised in John 10:10 means not just the 'good stuff' but a great variety, an abundance, of life experiences–the good and the bad. When we were married we promised "for better, for worse; for richer, for poorer; in sickness and in health". We had had years of 'better' and now we were having some 'worse'. All was well after all, though most days it didn't feel like it!

Since there was no therapy available for Paul I developed my own to try to help him escape from the 'ice cube' he was locked inside. I read to him a lot and tried to get him to talk to me. I would pretend I couldn't remember the meanings of two words that sounded quite similar to get him to 'explain' the difference. We still had a cow and chickens so at least twice a day he had to go outside the house to look after the animals. Sometimes he would come back to ask me what he was supposed to do outside but he would always go and do what was necessary. I had to make sure that Paul was never feeling that he was useless or disabled but at the same time he had to be protected from getting lost or hurt. That was very challenging. Perhaps the hardest part was that he knew perfectly well that there was something not right but he would not give in and just accept being disabled. He never once stopped trying to regain his strength and mental abilities. He never once stopped believing that his faithful Lord Jesus would heal him completely.

Our very busy lives, Paul's and mine, had come to an abrupt halt but our children's lives continued on without us. Jennifer eventually broke the relationship with the alcoholic boy-friend and completed her university studies to become a French teacher. She found a new boy-friend, a Muslim fellow student, who asked her to marry him. Heather got married and completed her nurses training. Peter finished High School, got a job and moved out of home also. The house felt very, very empty.

The Lord often uses very unconventional circumstances to reveal His truth. One afternoon I had a phone call from Peter who asked me to find a temporary bank card that he had left in a drawer in his former bedroom and to use it to get some money out of his account and pay a bill for him. He told me his password and where the bank was. I was most reluctant because I knew that I really did not have the authorization to get money from his account. However, being a 'helpful' mum I went off to do as he asked. I felt as though every policeman in town was watching me. My hands were shaking and I was very nervous. I put the card in and pressed the right buttons only to see it flash on the screen 'Invalid Card'. I snatched that thing from the machine and ran for my car. I was shaking all over and crying! This was much too much reaction. What was going on? I started to pray and felt the Lord ask "Why are you so upset? Why is it always so necessary for you to be good? Why can you not make mistakes?" As I sat and pondered His questions I remembered my Mum saying, "I'll love you if you're good." As I sat there I realized how much I was in bondage to 'being good'. The Lord quietly revealed to me all the ways that I had tried to cover mistakes and sins. I had not really trusted Jesus to do what He said He came to do–namely to rescue me from sin and separation from the Father. Oh I knew all the prayers and correct words but had not truly applied them to myself! I declared myself right there to be a SINNER. I started to laugh and by the time I got home I was almost shouting "I am a sinner! I am a sinner." Paul must have thought that I'd really gone 'over the edge' this time. At last I knew that Jesus came to save me, even me! The only requirement for being accepted by Jesus was to be a sinner and I qualified. I did not have to be good in order to get Jesus to love me.

I remembered when I was very young–maybe four or five years old–saying to my Mum, "Do you love me, Mummy?" And she replied, "I'll love you if you're good." Oh how I tried to be good! Who would love me or look after me if I wasn't good? When she died when I was 14 years old I wondered for a long time if I had been bad. I had to do everything right. I had to be good–so did my husband and my children and even the dog. We had to be **good**. I had also been very critical of other people who did not, in my opinion, keep the rules. I was frequently angry or impatient or anxious and too often it was more important to be right than to be compassionate and encouraging. My children remembered the criticism, anger and intolerance but not the times that I spent trying to help them with homework or making new clothes for them or driving them to school day after day. My relationship with them was based on correctness more than on unconditional love. They may not have been able to put it into those words exactly but that was the situation. In my ignorance I was eating from the 'tree of the knowledge of good and evil' and it had horribly poisoned my relationships with my precious children. I knew about Christian legalism but failed to recognize it in myself. In spite of my new knowledge though, that I am a sinner, it has taken a long time to change old habits, thought patterns and expectations.

What Paul and I had failed to understand is that it really isn't about keeping the rules as much as it is about motivation. There are at least four motivations for keeping the law. For example, Exodus 20:15 says "You shall not steal". The least important reason to keep that law is because I don't want to get caught. It's not a bad reason but it isn't great. Next is because it is the wrong thing to do. The conscience is a good guide after all. The third motivation is because I would not want to bring shame on my wonderful husband and family by breaking the law. Not wanting to hurt others is certainly better than just being afraid for my own skin if I get caught. But the best motivation is because I will do nothing to break the love and trust my heavenly Father has put into my life. Keeping His law is the most important motivation to keep me in right relationship with Him. It is not so much that I keep the law but that the law of God keeps me.

Sometimes things are so obvious we miss them. When Jesus taught His disciples to pray He started, "Our Father". That is a relationship. Jesus said over and over in many different ways that He and the Father are one. He called His disciples His 'brothers' in Matt 12:49 and said in John 15:15, "I have called you friends". Jesus urges us to love one another from a sincere heart. Relationship is written all over our scriptures. Jesus wants relationship because He came to bring a Kingdom that is based on relationship. We pray, "Thy kingdom come; thy will be done". That is not a passive prayer but a request to be included in the process of building God's kingdom here on earth. It is not saying "just let it drop down from the sky like gently falling rain, if you please sometime Lord". "Thy kingdom come" is a prayer that invites immediate warfare from the enemy whose own kingdom is threatened by relationships based on unconditional love. After His resurrection Jesus said very clearly and precisely in Matt 28:18; "All authority in heaven and on earth has been given to Me". He then said to His disciples that they were to go in the power and authority that He gave to them to defeat His enemy and to establish the kingdom of God through the power of the Holy Spirit. "Thy kingdom come".

God's kingdom is based in relationship and powered by authority. Too often we muddle authority with control. God gives us authority but never control. It was not until after the accident that Paul and I recognized the difference between the two. Paul came to understand that authority is delegated by one with power to enable a person to make decisions or carry out actions on behalf of others for the best good of others. Control makes decisions affecting others but mainly for one's own self-centred benefit. Too often we think that in order to have 'authority' it has to be because we have control over other people or things. I have come to think that because I belong to Jesus I have authority over my own domain and my domain is, at the very least, my space where I live. I am really thankful that I do not have control. I can determine whether my space, my home, will be filled with my faith in God or not. Will I be more concerned with being right or creating a safe non-critical place to grow? Will I be a happy person or not? I once heard a lady say that only I can decide whether I will be a happy little old lady or a miserable little old lady, but should the Lord tarry I WILL be a little old lady!

Women have authority from God in their homes. God planned it that way even though we don't always use it wisely or well. It is symbolized in Judaism by the woman of the home being given the task of lighting the Sabbath candles every week. It is one of her tasks, a privilege really, to keep alight the truth of God in the home. In Jewish thought, the wife IS the home. We are taught to submit to our husbands and too often that is translated in our Western understanding to mean 'Let the man make the decisions, have his own way and the wife needs just to be obedient.' That is a very inadequate understanding of submitting to a spouse. If you 'submit' an application or report you are giving your input, your thoughts, and your suggestions to be considered in the making of a decision. You become part of the process. You have that authority. God called us as women to be the 'ezer knegdo' which is (badly) translated as a 'helpmate' as has been mentioned before in previous chapters. The ezer knegdo is supposed to identify the enemy, identify his tactics and help to develop a strategy to defeat those tactics. Ultimately the man has the responsibility of making the final decision but if the woman fails to take her proper place of helping to form that decision his task is made much harder. Galatians 6:2 tells us to "Carry one another's burdens and so fulfil the law of Christ". This principle applies to all relationship, especially marriages. All friendships need mutual support to be able to defeat satan's schemes.

Paul and I have made a point of studying the Jewish roots of our Christian faith. In one of the books the point was made that the early church was based mainly in the home because the principle place of the Jewish faith was not in the synagogue but in the home. Shabbat every Friday around the family table with all the prayers, blessings and teaching accomplished many things that we have largely lost. Every child was blessed individually and the mother of the home was honoured by her husband in the presence of the children by the reading as a prayer, of Proverbs 31. Both parents but especially the father took a place of leadership in the teaching of Torah and training the children for adulthood.

When the new 'Messianic movement' looked for leaders there were many because the fathers were already able to take that role in their families. When I was a young girl there was a saying that I heard frequently–"The family that prays together stays together". Because the family was such a strong, stable element in the new faith of Christianity the Romans were not able to stamp out either Christianity or Judaism. That principle holds true to this day for the Jews around the world and also for Christians in places like China and North Korea where there is much persecution. A church building is easy to destroy but if the faith is dispersed into many homes it can and will survive.

Another overlooked positive outcome of such a simple thing as weekly prayer and blessing of children is that the children become much more successful in life. There is a spiritual power in spoken words. It isn't a hard and fast rule, but it seems more than a coincidence that more than 10 percent of the medical and scientific Nobel prizes have gone to Jews who make up only one tenth of one percent of the world's population. Relationship in families seems to be very important indeed in God's kingdom plans.

We have not appreciated the extent of God's relationship intentions. I want to quote from the daily devotional we use called Every Day With Jesus.

"Dr E. Stanley Jones defined Christianity as 'the science of relating well to others in the spirit of Jesus.' He also said that 'we are as mature as our relationships'. Unless we learn to relate to others in the way the members of the Trinity relate to each other–in other 'centeredness'–we may well find our union somewhat blocked. C. S. Lewis described the church as a laboratory in which we have the opportunity to fine-tune our relationships." End quote.

God means for us to be very involved–in fact interdependent–with each other and with Him. We live in a society based on individualism unfortunately, thanks to the pervasive influence of ancient Greek philosophy or Hellenism. We have come to expect that even very close relationships are not necessarily to be trusted or expected to be dependable or permanent. Consider the divorce rate in this country or the number of children who are out of relationship with their families. It is an epidemic. But Jesus has given us the most incredible invitation. Not only are we to be His friends, we are invited to be His prayer partners in bringing His kingdom to earth.

Recently when I was 'complaining' to the Lord about some of my prayers not being answered and wondering when it would be my turn, He gave me the following wonderful insight. He said, "Do you remember when your friend Susannah was so ill and unable to do anything for herself? Do you remember that everything she needed–antibiotics, saline, nutrition, everything came to her intravenously? A nurse had to make sure that the amount was correctly flowing and sometimes at different rates for different solutions. When one little bag was empty another had to be put in place. The nurse had to sign a form and double check that it was the correct medication. Prayer is like that. Sometimes it only takes one injection–sometimes days or weeks of little bags. BUT...if you add doubt, or worry, or fear, or judgement or any other negative to your prayer you contaminate what is in the little bag!" From that illustration I also realized that the treatments went directly into Susannah's blood adding more understanding about the nature of our blood in our bodies.

I also saw how God plans for us to be interconnected. We are truly interdependent, far more than we usually realize. A number of scripture verses took on new meaning and understanding, almost like God delights in shining different coloured lights on passages that have become too familiar. For example, Eph. 3:18, "I pray also that the eyes of your heart may be enlightened in order that you may know the hope to which He has called you, the riches of His glorious inheritance in the saints, and His incompararably great power for us who believe." Col. 1:10, "And we pray this in order that you may live a life worthy of the Lord and may please Him in every way: bearing fruit in every good work, growing in the knowledge of God, being strengthened with all power according to His glorious might so that you may have great endurance and patience, and joyfully giving thanks to the Father, who has qualified you to share in the inheritance of the saints in the kingdom of light." Phil. 4:6 "Do not be anxious about anything, but in everything by prayer and petition, with thanksgiving, present your requests to God." One of my favourite stories in Luke 8:50 is, "Jesus said to Jairus "Don't be afraid; just believe and she will be healed."

God goes much further than just giving us scripture promises, authority to work with Him, personal promises and friendships. God takes an even more massive risk. He makes a covenant with us. In

our culture we don't have much of an appreciation of all the implications of a covenantal relationship. We understand contracts fairly well, particularly if we have ever taken out a loan, bought a house or employed someone to do repairs on something we own. A covenant is much more binding. There are at least eight elements to a covenant.
1. We exchange weapons.
2. We exchange coats.
3. We exchange names.
4. We mix blood by cutting our wrists or arms and mingling blood.
5. We make a scar.
6. We exchange tokens.
7. We have a meal together and share bread and wine.
8. We establish a memorial.

In our everyday lives some of those elements don't look very familiar until we seek some clarification. In 1Sam 18:3 we read, "And Jonathan made a covenant with David because he loved him as himself. Jonathan took off the robe he was wearing and gave it to David, along with his tunic and even his sword, his bow and his belt." In other words he was saying, 'Between us there are no weapons pointed at each other and everything that covers me is to cover you also.' In Eph 6 we read that we are to put on the whole armour of God that the Holy Spirit will give us to defeat God's enemy. We will also be given new robes of righteousness in Rev 6:11. We will also be given a new name according to Revelation 2:17. For women this is very real as we receive a new name when we enter into the covenant of marriage. Although most of us don't have to cut our wrists or arms to establish a covenant there is still the issue of blood when a virgin marries. There is a story told of the missionary Dr Livingston who journeyed through Africa. He made covenant with many tribes and had the scars on his arms to prove it. When he met a new tribe he would hold up his arms and they would see all the scars and realize that this small defenceless white man had a great many covenant partners behind him, and that it would probably be a good idea not to tangle with him. Those scars were made by rubbing ash into the cuts that were made to allow the blood to be mingled. It seems rather barbaric to our Western sensibilities but this is still done in many places in the world. The tokens we share can be as simple as a ring which we do in a marriage ceremony or as heart wrenching as exchanging children as some primitive tribes still do. You think more than twice if attacking your enemy is going to harm your own child. When we go out for a meal in many restaurants the first thing we are asked as we sit down is, "Can I bring you something to drink?" and then some bread is also brought to the table. Having a meal together especially with bread and wine is very familiar to us but we seldom consciously make the connection that our communion service is really the celebration of the new covenant that Jesus established with His followers. He even said "This is the blood of the new covenant, which is poured out for many" in Luke 22:20. Further He said to do this as often as we drink it, and we have a memorial, a feast, an anniversary.

There are severe penalties for breaking a covenant. In Jer 31:3, God says, "I have loved you with a everlasting love". If God breaks that promise He says there are consequences for Himself as well as for us. He has put His very life on the line for us from before the beginning. He cannot and will not break covenant. If we truly know Him and love Him we won't either.

There are four major covenants in the Bible: the Abrahamic covenant, the Mosaic covenant, the Davidic covenant, and the Messianic covenant. Three of those have been fulfilled for the most part but the fourth has yet to happen. That covenant is the Davidic covenant. David was promised that one of his own descendents would sit on his throne forever. We believe that that man is Jesus, Yeshua in Hebrew. Jesus was crucified as King of the Jews according to the inscription that Herod had placed over the cross. At the time His 'scriptural role' was as the suffering servant, the lamb of God. When He returns it will not be as a baby again, nor as a servant, but as the King of the Jews and even more importantly as the King of Kings. If He is to be a King then He must have a kingdom. That is why the re-establishment of Israel, with Hebrew speaking Jews is so important and prophetic. The King of the Jews must have Jews in the land to be king over. There must also be an understanding among those Jews that they have an inheritance to share with all the nations that will make their King to be King of Kings.

We need to return to the formula we started with; R + R–R = R&R. We are very familiar–too familiar–with the rules and regulations part. We absolutely must re-establish the missing ingredient of relationship into our lives. Enough with individualism! We talk glibly about fellowship in our churches. We even designate a room or rooms to be called the Fellowship Room. The word 'fellowship' is so much more than tea or coffee on a Sunday morning. It comes from the old Anglo Saxon word "fell monger"–one who deals in hides. In Medieval times the village people would herd their cattle all together on communal land near the village. Their cattle constituted their wealth because the prosperity of the whole community depended on mutual trust and provision. They had to live relationships that worked. Our early settlers in this country also knew how to have close relationships. The whole community participated at harvest time. It was work but it was also fun. There was laughter and games and when harvest was done there was a party in the school house. Everybody was there. The babies slept under the tables and desks and the adults danced to their own community musicians. There was always a fiddle, often an accordian and we all sang.

We have been called to be part of the establishment of the kingdom of God on earth. It is a priviledge and a huge task. We begin by loving Jesus with our hearts and growing to love one another wholeheartedly.

Chapter 6

DEVELOPING INTIMACY

Relationships built on interdependency are almost totally foreign to our Western mindsets and training. The 'self-made' man or woman is held up as someone to be emulated and honoured. We look back at our pioneers and see them as very independent tough folks who were very capable and innovative in all sorts of difficult circumstances.

In 2007 I went with three friends, Stewart and Janet Wilson and Susannah Andersen, to Israel to attend a conference sponsored by the Knesset Christian Allies Caucus entitled 'A Women's Summit'. We learned more about how women all over the world are mistreated than I thought possible. The capacity for creating evil and harm is truly impressive and totally diabolical! During a radio interview one morning before we went to the Conference, I heard a discussion with some women in India who had been talking to women in North America. The Indian women asked "How do you deal with girls"? It turned out that what they were really asking was "Do you abort girl babies or just let them die after birth"? How do we find a basis for relationship with such a totally foreign way of thinking? Where do we even start? Where can we find common ground with women who are trying to deal with so-called 'honour killing', female genital mutilation, female infanticide or being forced into marriage at age 10? There are so many places in the world where it is not safe to be a woman. I am so very thankful that I was born in Canada at such a time as this.

The trip started with a week-long tour of mostly Northern Israel. Our Tour Guide was a History professor, Izzy Naaman, who also worked as a guide when he was not teaching. He had never led a group of women before, especially a group of Christian women. During the course of the week we introduced him to many places in Israel that he had never visited before as he was an Orthodox Jew. One afternoon we went to a lovely church in Jerusalem called St Peter in Gallicantu. We went up to the roof of the church where we had a view of the Temple Mount and one of the tour leaders told us that that was where Abraham had taken Isaac to be sacrificed. God had stopped Abraham from killing his son and provided the ram caught by its horns in a thicket. She then said that the thorns were like a 'crown of thorns' similar to what had been put on Jesus' head when He was on the cross. That was obviously a new and shocking thought to Izzy and he looked like he had been punched in the stomach. He was pretty quiet for the rest of the time on that roof. Evidently his thinking was being challenged.

After a couple of days he said that a number of people had been asking him about his family and what it was like to live and work in Israel. He said he had never been asked those questions before by a tour group but those are questions that are important to women. He opened up more and more and shared with us about his three kids who had all served in the Israel Defence Force, the IDF, where he lived and many other details of life in the Land.

At the end of the week, a tour guide is usually very ready to go home to see his own family but Izzy seemed very reluctant to say goodbye. He stayed to have dinner and continued to talk and share well into the evening. We had invited him into our world and, fleeting though it was, we had built a relationship, however brief.

It is probably very obvious but men and women develop relationships very differently. Women are more focused on personal details and men want to know about activity details. As I was preparing, I asked a few people, both men and women, what they wanted to know when they first meet someone. The person's name is most obvious but then other details were quite different. Some women wanted to know "who else do you know?, are you married or single, do you have children?, where do you come from?". But men wanted to know "the person's occupation, purpose for being here, what sort of character is this"? Women tend to deduce character from more personal questions and men are much more direct and literal in their interactions. It all gets even more complicated when a man and a woman are meeting for the first time!

I want to share with you a couple of examples. One day, when I was much younger, a young man came into the bank where I was working. It was lunch time which was the only time I had to wait on customers as most of the time I worked behind the scenes. The man wanted to know if his money had arrived from New Zealand and how to open an account. In the course of the next few minutes I learned his name, address, reason for being in Canada, where he had come from, marital status as well as how much money he actually had. I opened his account, gave him a cheque book and a passbook, said goodbye and 'welcome to Canada'. As far as I knew that was the end of the relationship. But he had other ideas. He came into the bank again the next day and asked to speak to me though it was not lunch time that day. Since I had been so helpful the previous day he asked for some help with other details that had arisen as he was trying to get registered at UBC. He needed a doctor's certificate and asked if I could give him the name of a doctor so he could complete his registration process. I gave him my own doctor's name and again thought that that was the end. Predictably perhaps, he came in again the next day with another question and I began to get the idea that this man was lonely. The term had not yet started and there were no other students in residence yet at the university so new contacts for him were very few. So, being a good Christian girl, I invited him to go to church with me on Sunday. I arranged where we could meet and said goodbye–again. Only later did it occur to me–slow learner that I am–that I would probably be expected to spend the rest of the day with a man I really did not know. In a bit of a panic I phoned my pastor's wife and explained what I had done. Her immediate response was "You had better bring him home with us after church for dinner." Whew! God bless her!

Now at this point things got a little complicated because I had been going out for the previous four years with a man who also worked at the bank. He had just resigned his position to go back to university to become a doctor. Before term started he had gone for a short holiday and it was while he was away that I invited this stranger to go to church with me. When I look back on it now I think the Lord must have been having quite a chuckle–at our expense. I was perfectly honest with both men and, believe it or not, they met one day on campus and agreed–both of them–to court me and as the saying goes–may the best man win. So for a few weeks my life was a bit of a whirlwind. Lunches, concerts, long walks, church gatherings, dances made for a very busy time. Both men were very godly Christian men. Both were headed for very wonderful professional careers. It became very obvious that I was going to have to make a choice as to which one I would marry since that was their intention. By this time I had a long and very healthy relationship with the man I had known for four years and he knew everything about me. However he had not asked me to marry him in four years of close friendship. The man from New Zealand, on the other hand, made me laugh–and he did ask me to marry him, fortunately before we all died of exhaustion!! The acid test of the relationship came when I had to tell my new fiancé about a terrible episode in my life. I had been locked in a room and raped and had become pregnant when I was 18 years old. With many tears I had given my little boy up for adoption. I fully expected Paul to reject me when I told him my very sad story but instead he just held me close and reassured me that whatever was past could stay there and that he loved me for who I was now. The next day he appeared at the bank carrying a box with a dozen long stemmed red roses. We have been married now for over 50 years. We are both still very close friends with my other gentleman friend, who did indeed become a doctor, and I love his wife like she was my own sister. God is so very good.

Once the decision had been made, quite a number of things changed very quickly. At the time I probably didn't examine them as closely as I am doing now. Some of the changes were obvious but many were subtle. I didn't go out nearly as often and when I did it was always with Paul. I was introduced to a whole new group of people including an old New Zealand friend of Paul's who had also come to UBC to study. Paul and Les had been at school together in Wellington and at University there as well. I found I was always listening for Paul's voice which I began to be able to pick out even in a crowd. Gradually I could recognize his footsteps and his shape when he was walking on the street especially if he was coming towards me.

My own hopes and dreams and ambitions began to change as well. I was very much a city girl. Paul was very much an outdoorsman. I quickly learned that if I didn't want to spend a lot of time alone I had better learn to appreciate and enjoy the things he was interested in. When we met I couldn't have told you the difference between a cedar tree and a Douglas fir. But I learned. He was taking many wildlife courses so I helped him to study. In the process I learned also how to recognize different ducks, swans, geese and other birds. It was really important to him that I become comfortable in his world and he was a very patient teacher. This was not always a comfortable or simple process though. There was one memorable day when we had a certain disagreement about just how far I was willing to compromise on critters in the house. It was shortly after we got married that I came home from work to find a garter snake in a plastic bag in the fridge. You see Paul had never seen a snake before as there are no snakes in New Zealand and when he found this snake he brought it home and put it in the fridge to see if he could induce it to hibernate!! Thanks to my fear of snakes the experiment failed!

I had had great hopes of becoming a teacher but I put my ambitions on hold to help him achieve his goals. It was not a sacrifice on my part. I just felt that when Paul was finished his forestry degree then it would be my turn

Now I can see how this process was so very like what happens when our lives become focused on Jesus. Our hopes and dreams for our lives in this world become so much less important as we begin to fall in love with our Lord and desire to help Him build His kingdom on earth as it is in heaven. We start to be able to recognize His voice, we listen for His step, and do things that we know will please Him. It is not that we cease to be who we are–I am still Shirley–but my desires are no longer the main focus of my life. That probably sounds very contradictory but I become more than who I was before as now I have another person who is a very vital part of me and of my life.

The second relationship I want to share is very different. On March 24, 1997 I received a phone call that threw my life into terrible chaos. Not even my wildest dreams prepared me for that call. A man's voice that I didn't recognize asked me "Are you Shirley Louise Streeter?" "Yes." "And did you grow up in North Vancouver?" "Yes." I couldn't think who this could be but I had been to a school reunion a few months earlier so I thought it might be an old school friend. "I need to ask you this next question. Did you ever give up a child for adoption?" In the awful silence that followed the man's voice said "I am your son". I have never felt so shocked. Surely the roof would collapse any second.

At the other end of the phone my "son" was tremendously excited. He kept saying "I can't believe I've found you." Neither could I! I heard myself ask "How did you find me?" It seems that the adoption laws had been changed a few months earlier and it was no longer necessary to have both parties agree before information could be released. He had simply applied for my information and then, thanks to Google, started to call all the Streeters listed in phone books in B.C. He found one of my cousins who referred him to an aunt and that was how he got my married name and where I live. One of the first things he said was "Thank you for giving me life and not aborting me." I was totally shocked by such a response! He also asked if he had any siblings? Nothing could have prepared me for that question. The dynamics of our family could never be the same again! After exchanging a few details of our lives he promised to call again the next day. Only after he hung up did I realize that I hadn't asked him his name.

I didn't sleep much that night. So many memories. So many fears. Boy, were there a lot of fears. All through that long dark night I relived that terrible day when I was locked in a room and couldn't get out. I have no memory of how I got home. When I found that I was pregnant I just wanted to die. I thought of suicide several times. I was certain that my life was over. Shame! Guilt! Fear of rejection! Hopelessness! Feeling dirty somehow! I had suppressed it all for years, and intimacy–especially sexual intimacy–had been a real struggle for such a long time. Sometime close to morning I heard the gentle still small voice of the Lord say "You need to separate the child from the event."

I could have refused to have anything to do with him, but his words "thank you for not aborting me" had been spoken in such an honouring way. I could have refused to introduce him to our children who knew nothing about him. With considerable trepidation and with Paul's full blessings, I allowed the door to relationship to open. This began a long and continuing process of separating the child from the event. I had given my baby the name Mark but this man, who is my son, was named James. Jay was what he liked to be called. His first words to me on that initial phone call were honouring words, thanking me for giving him life. Now I needed to find new life for myself too.

Jay is my son but he was never my child. I never wiped away his tears, or helped him with school homework, or watched him playing sports. I prayed for him many times at many different stages of his life but from a great distance and without first hand knowledge. There are many missing parts of this relationship with a grown man who is my son but not my child. Sometimes he calls me Shirley and sometimes he calls me Mother. There are no models to help us figure out what this relationship should look like. We are having to forge our own model–and from a distance of many miles.

In several ways this is also similar to building a relationship with Jesus. He lives in heaven and I live on earth. God is my Father, Jesus is my Brother, my Friend, my Saviour but there are many gaps in my experience of Him since I can't see Him or touch Him or even hear Him often.

In many ways it is like having a pen pal, a friend you only knew through letters. Perhaps the modern equivalent is Facebook. There has to be an exchange of letters that discuss thoughts, ideas, questions, hopes, dreams, activities and all kinds of other details about the lives of the participants in order to establish a friendship that can continue to grow and develop. In many ways our relationship with Jesus is very like that. When we keep a journal or record our prayers and interactions with the Lord it is as if He becomes a pen pal of sorts. Just as we can't remember every conversation we have with our spouse or parents or friends so we will not remember the things the Lord tells us either if we don't write it down. Journaling is a discipline but don't let that word fool you. When you realize that you are simply recording the conversation of One who loves you with an everlasting love simply for who you are and not what you do, it becomes a pleasure and not a chore. Journaling is really just writing love letters to Jesus and can make that love relationship much more tangible. It will not be intellectual only as Jesus is a very passionate Person. Conversations with Him will be full of humour as well as seriousness; playfulness as well as giving challenging direction.

At one point our son Peter re-dedicated his life to the Lord. When his wife Shauna asked him what he was going to do next he was a bit defensive at first. When she said that she just wanted to know how to pray for him he said he would just have to get back to reading his Bible. He also expressed a great desire to "just have a cup of coffee with Jesus". That is a great place to start to keep a journal–share a cup of coffee with Jesus and write.

Your journal may even bring much healing to you. A few years ago my friend Susannah was desperately ill and nearly died. Following some very complicated surgery she couldn't remember how to pray or even who Jesus is. Her husband John brought her own journals to her in the hospital and she could read, in her own handwriting, wonderful long interactions with her Lord. That was such an important key to her recovery from major surgery and several strokes. I am constantly humbled at her faithfulness in keeping her journal with Jesus.

As well as a very vibrant prayer life, keeping a journal and fellowshipping with other Christians, most of us have learned to read our Bibles regularly. Some people find such a discipline very dry and boring and no wonder. There is no other book or magazine that we ever read that we just read a sentence here, a paragraph there or a whole chapter and expect to get the whole story. Early in our Christian adventure we heard John Paul Jackson teach about "reading the white parts" of our Bibles.–another way of saying "reading between the lines". The illustration he used was from the book of Acts where it says in chapter 2:14 that Peter stood up and addressed the crowd. The question that John Paul asked was "why does it say that Peter stood up"? Because obviously, he was lying down. So why was he lying down? Because he was overwhelmed by the Holy Spirit. John Paul was getting us to think past the little black letters that were written/printed on the page. We need to be able to put ourselves into the scenes and ask a whole lot of questions to fill out the story in colour and not just see black letters on a white page.

Let me give you an illustration. In Genesis 3:8 God calls to the man person and says "Where are you?" Now God knew perfectly well where Adam was but what we need to think about is what did God's voice sound like? Was He angry? Accusing? Worried? Impatient? Or was He sorrowful? Wistful? Sad? Hurt? What does His voice sound like in your ears? What do you think Adam heard? Did Adam's guilt cause him to misunderstand and be defensive, to try to shift the blame and thereby miss the opportunity to confess his sin and be rehabilitated? Was Adam's sin really, not so much disobedience of God's command not to eat of the tree of the knowledge of good and evil, as saying to God, in effect, "You did a lousy job of providing a wife for me." If you are like me then you have probably been taught that it was disobedience, the breaking of God's law, that caused God to kick the first couple out of the Garden.

However if we read this carefully it seems more like the original sin was really accusing God of wrong doing. Can you hear the anguish in God's voice when He asks "What have you done?" I feel that when I try to hear what God's voice really sounds like at that moment it is full of extreme sorrow. I feel He is expressing great pain and anguish because the fellowship they had all enjoyed was now shattered and broken. The worst part, from God's point of view, was that Adam and Eve didn't even realize how terribly they had hurt

Him! They lapsed into bickering, blame-shifting. There isn't even a hint of repentance on their part in the conversation.

Unquestionably, God had known from the beginning that such a calamity was possible–even probable. So "from <u>before</u> the creation of the world" it tells us in 1 Peter 1:20 the Father, Son and Holy Spirit had agreed upon a plan of redemption for the precious sons and daughters that God had created. First though, Adam and Eve had to be removed from the Garden. The Lord took an animal and killed it. He then used the skin to make coverings, clothing to hide the nakedness of the man and woman. It was not so much to keep them warm as to cover them with the "blood of the lamb" and from the gaze of Satan! In the process the first couple learned about offering a sacrifice of blood to cover their sins. It is questionable whether they understood the full implications of what God had just done. It is very clear though, that when we see their two sons bringing sacrifices to worship God that the lesson had been learned when we read that Abel brought the fat portions of his flock which was an acceptable offering. We know that the need for blood was certainly passed on to the next generation.

Once Adam and his wife had learned about the need for blood sacrifice they were taken to the edge of the Garden and sent out to earn their living by the sweat of their brow. God then instructed his trusted Cherubim to guard the way to the entrance so that the couple could not get back in. You see, there were **TWO** trees in the Garden and having eaten of the wrong tree they must not eat of the Tree of Everlasting Life as they would then have had eternal life–but in eternal sin. The thought of His precious children living forever separated from all hope of reconciliation was too much for God to bear. As He was instructing His angels He said "The man has become like one of Us, knowing good and evil. Now therefore, to prevent his putting out his hand and taking also from the Tree of Life, eating and living forever ......" The thought was so terrible to God that He couldn't finish the sentence. His tender heart was broken!

Since that day, relationships, as we can all attest, have not been easy. Adam and Eve understood very well the need for obedience. All of us have also been taught that it is utterly essential to obey God's laws or things will not go well for us. The thing that I missed–and perhaps you might have too–was that a relationship with God was not only possible but also was based first of all on **HIS** love for me much more than my obedience to His laws and decrees. It is a love-based relationship He offers not an obedience-based one.

The failure of people to understand and appreciate God's motivations is never more evident than at Mount Sinai. Moses had demonstrated by his life and actions that he had a close personal relationship with the God named in Hebrew YHWH, usually rendered either Yahweh or Yehovah. When he led the people out of their slavery in Egypt it was clear that God was working through Moses. Every plague that was manifested was directed against an object of Egyptian worship–flies, frogs, the Nile, the sun, the whole lot including the first born (Ex 14:31). The Red Sea parted, the soldiers drowned, even water came bubbling from a rock to prove that Moses was in touch with a power none of them could explain away. When it came time to <u>personally</u> meeting that mighty God who was going out of His way to provide for them, they fled in terror. Why? They had been warned to prepare themselves, to wash their clothes, not to touch the mountain or to go past the pillars that had been set up and they were all obedient to those orders. They had been given every possible warning that they should expect a most unusual experience.

So why did they flee? In Ex 20:18 our English Bibles say that there was thunder, lightning, a trumpet, and much trembling. In Hebrew it says that the people heard "many voices" coming from the mountain. Those voices spoke words that the people could understand. God was talking to them. The words suggest that there were different languages that the different peoples who had joined up with the former Israeli slaves on their exodus could identify and understand. None of the gods they had been used to in Egypt had been able to talk and this was terrifying. I suspect that if we heard a very loud disembodied voice talking to us with words from a smoke-enshrouded mountain, and trumpets blowing we also would be terrified and run away!

I have had an experience sort of like that though not nearly as dramatic. As I mentioned in Chapter 1, in 1979 when I needed surgery on my hands to relieve carpel tunnel syndrome I prayed for the Lord to help me (not necessarily to heal me) because I was afraid to have somebody cut my hands. The Lord didn't just give me peace as I asked and hoped He would. He healed my hands without surgery. It was wonderful and I was relieved, thrilled, amazed and very bewildered. What kind of God is this who can just say "Be healed" and it is done? What else could He do that I knew nothing about? Even more, what else _would_ He do that would turn my life in directions I couldn't even imagine? If my reaction was confusion–and I knew all the stories of Jesus' miracles of healing, turning water to wine and calming storms–what must it have been like for the former slaves standing before a smoking, trembling mountain that was blowing trumpets and speaking words?

Time and time again the Lord sent prophets and psalmists, priests and teachers all through the Old Testament period to reassure the people that His nature was love. He used innumerable examples and situations to try to make them understand that His laws were only to keep them from harm, sickness and terrible consequences. Prophets, judges, kings and psalmists laid before the people a great promise of redemption, a messiah, and a complete restoration of all that had been lost in the Garden of Eden.

We need to look at a few of those scriptures. We'll start with Jer 31:3. The Lord declares through Jeremiah that in spite of all their suffering, disobedience and rebellion He has not stopped loving them. As He promises them total restoration it is based on His love alone. Not only has He always loved them but He is going to woo them, to draw them to Himself because His great desire for them is for their joy and well-being. Almost the whole of the 31st chapter of Jeremiah is filled with the Lord's eager anticipation of what it will be like when the people He loves so much are reconciled with Him. Like their forebears in the wilderness they don't understand. To this day they see the wilderness time as punishment and the exile times as God's abandonment of His so-called Chosen People.

From God's point of view the forty years they spent in the wilderness became a time of training. They had to learn how to become a nation together instead of a group of former slaves who needed to be ordered what to do and when to do it. In the wilderness they learned strategy, leadership, co-operative government and diplomacy, as well as dependence on God.

One of my favourite passages of scripture is Jer 29:10-14. Yahweh tells Jeremiah to send a letter of encouragement to the people who had been carried into exile by Nebuchadnezzar telling them that God knew the plans He had for them, plans for good and not for evil meant to prosper them. Further more when they are restored to His Land they will seek Him and they will find Him simply because that is the desire of His heart. God tells them ahead of time that they will be restored not because of their obedience but because it is His plan. He has been consistent from the very beginning that it is never salvation by our works, be they obedience, sacrifices, buildings or anything else. It is always, and only, based on His loving plans.

In 1 Chron 28:9 King David assures his son Solomon that "if he seeks the Lord his God and serves Him with wholehearted devotion the Lord will be found by him". Some translations say "If you search for Him He will let you find Him". That same promise is repeated in 2 Chron 15:2 when the prophet Azariah met with King Asa and the people of Judah and Benjamin

In the New Testament it becomes even clearer. In 1 John 4:19 it says "We love because He first loved us." It was not something we chose to initiate. We can only respond. God loved us FIRST and we can choose to accept that as a gift and return His love by loving Him back....or not! He does not force or coerce. When we do love Him we will desire with everything we have and are to please Him, obey His commands, and be in His presence at every opportunity. Earlier in John's gospel Jesus says to all His disciples "I do not say that I shall pray to the Father for you, for the Father loves you Himself, because you have loved Me and believed that I came from God."

I want to go back to Moses at Mt Sinai again for a moment. There was something else that happened there that is still having a considerable effect on us even today. When the people ran away they said to Moses "you go and talk to God for us. We're too scared of Him". They set up a mediation system where Moses or later the priests would go before the Lord and then tell the people what God had said this time. Such a system removed the possibility of a close intimate relationship with God for almost the whole community. It would be a bit like needing a mediator in a marriage to enable the two partners to have a relationship. There would be very little meaningful communication in such a marriage, no satisfaction and I cannot even imagine how there could ever be children.

Even today in many Christian churches the expectation is for the priest or minister to have all the words from God and the people to passively receive whatever is delivered. In some denominations only the ordained clergy can bless the elements for communion or perform the sacraments. This has resulted in a people who have little or no expectation of God either speaking to them, working wonders through them or accepting them as worthy to be His friends and co-workers. I thank God that this is changing ever more quickly as the Lord reveals His nature to us. Still, for the most part, we are much too passive especially when it comes to sharing our faith with others who don't yet know Jesus.

In Ps 103:7 David wrote that "the Lord revealed His character to Moses, His deeds to the people of Israel." Now for a very long time I read that as being parallel–His character and His deeds being the same but it really isn't. God's character tells of His motivations, His plans and intentions–the 'why' of God–whereas His deeds are the product of His character–the 'what' of God. Because Moses had spent so much time just seeking God for who He is, he had the privilege of an intimate relationship with Him. David, also another shepherd, had spent many hours meditating on who God is and then was able to put his discoveries and insights into magnificent poetry to inspire and instruct us 3,000 years later.

How much expectation do we have that God will reveal Himself to us individually and personally? In John 17:3 Jesus said: "Now this is eternal life: that they may know you, the only true God, and Jesus Christ whom you have sent." All of us are anticipating eternal life. Can we truly say we KNOW both God and Jesus as David wrote about Moses? In the 6th verse of John 17 Jesus said "I have revealed You (or Your Name) to those You gave me out of the world." It is only in intimate relationships that such revelations occur. Can we really say that we know God's character, His motivations, plans and intentions?

I have made an awful discovery. From the time I was very little I have lived life from my own point of view. I could choose to be a friend–or not. I could choose to reach out to others–or not. I could choose to see a different point of view–or not. I could choose to love God–or not. The choice was mine. The truth is that God loves me whether I love Him or not. That is the heart of the whole issue of whether I will live from earth to heaven or heaven to earth. If I claim to love Jesus and desire an intimate relationship with Him then I have to give up my right to choose whether to follow Him or not. If I expect eternal life on Jesus' terms I must love Him in return, seek His face, hear His voice and do what He needs me to do to help establish His kingdom.

A while ago as I was preparing to share with a group of women from a book on intimacy I ran into a brick wall. The Lord told me very clearly that I could not teach something I was not prepared to do. One afternoon I was really struggling to hear the Lord and getting nowhere. I was very frustrated and getting angry. How could the Lord ask me to lead this weekend if He wouldn't show up? Then I heard a very quiet little voice say "When you dance with your Partner you have to let Him lead." Ouch! It can't be on my terms but only on His terms of total and mutual unconditional love. I cannot 'manage' this relationship. I can only respond to His love.

Let's go back to the thought of 'reading the white parts of scripture' and have a look at the Last Supper because I am fully convinced that the disciples and women around Jesus were no different in their humanity than we are. Let's set the stage. We know that the disciples and Jesus lay on their sides to eat around a triclinium–a three sided very low table. We have a pretty good idea of what they were eating and those of us who have attended a seder meal will be able to recognize the menu. When Jesus said that He was going away, what do you think the disciples felt? What did they say? What did they think? Even after three years of intimate friendship with Jesus, were they any better at accepting His agenda than I am? Or you are? How did they cope with their confusion and disappointment? When they heard Jesus say that He was going to the Father did their ears hear sorrow or excitement in His voice? What do you hear in His voice when you read about all the conversation at the Last Supper?

One afternoon I was reading those wonderful chapters in John again and I realized that so much of that conversation was really about Jesus trying to get His friends to move beyond their own perceptions and to see far beyond the present. The disciples looked for a messiah who would break the Roman bondage–a short-term political solution–but Jesus had a much bigger vision. How could He tell them about a Diaspora that would take them to the four corners of the world when they could barely imagine the distance to Rome? Or that nearly two thousand years would go by full of wars and much persecution of Jews and many others and still Messiah not be back? The weapons of war would move from swords and spears to chemicals, tanks, jet aircraft and deadly missiles. Jesus was able to see far, far into the future but it would not have made any sense to those friends gathered with Him that night. To us also Jesus alone knows what is coming. Perhaps it is a mercy that we are not able to see that far ahead. We can however, know with absolute certainty, that Jesus will walk with us every step of the way, neither leaving us nor abandoning us until all His kingdom plans are totally complete and He returns to earth.

Chapter 7

CALLED, EQUIPPED AND SENT OUT

Have you ever tried to sit before Jesus and ponder what it means to be His Betrothed. This has been a bit of a mystery to me–how I can be in an intimate relationship with Someone who is also intimate with billions of other people at the same time? The whole concept of a corporate Bride is very challenging. Many times I can't see myself able to be near my Beloved. I feel like I must be in a shadow in the back row somewhere. When I questioned the Lord He replied "Have you ever seen a garden with only one flower? Or a jewel with only one facet? Is there only one star in the sky? Are any of the flowers or stars lost in shadows?" "For your thoughts are not My thoughts says the Lord, neither are your ways My ways." (Isa 55:8) It doesn't quite answer my question but it does tell me that there are mysteries that I simply must trust to Jesus. I suppose it is just as well that there are many things left that we don't know because we are going to have eternity to discover so many new things about the Lover of our souls.

This quest was started by asking the question, "Whose daughter are you?" In Genesis 24 there is a very interesting story that we need to look at more closely. Abraham had sent his servant Eliezer to go to Haran to find a bride for Isaac. The second part of that servant's name should ring some bells for us. El**iezer** means 'My God helps'; so Abraham sent a man with a very prophetic name, to go to find a bride from his father's family. After travelling a very long time Eliezer arrived at the well near the town and found a girl, who was very beautiful, who was willing to draw water for his camels. In verse 23 Eliezer asked her, "Whose daughter are you?" His next question is very important. "Please tell me, is there room for us to lodge in your father's house?" It is very easy to skip past this point without understanding the importance of this question. When we know <u>whose</u> daughter we are, we will then realize that we have authority to welcome people into our Father's house. It is important to note also, that this particular daughter was to be the bride of the inheritor of the covenant God had made with Abraham. The father/daughter relationship, that for many of us has been a fractured and fractious struggle, is vital to the building of the Kingdom of God in all its fullness.

None of us has had perfect parents nor are we perfect parents ourselves either. It doesn't seem fair somehow that the way we related to our parents has such an effect on how we relate to our heavenly Father. God takes very seriously His command to, "Honour your father and your mother, that your days may be prolonged in the land which the Lord your God gives you." (Ex20:12) It is the first command with a promise attached. I have prayed through many tearful sessions of my own and with others, who have had parents who rejected them, were violent, absent, alcoholics, neglectful or just plain incompetent. Yet still God demands that we 'honour' father and mother. The question is usually the same "How can I do that when they don't deserve honour?" The only answer that comes anywhere near making sense is, "You need to salute the uniform" to use a military analogy.

Recently I was praying with a lady who had been sexually abused when she was only six years old. She told her mother but her mother did not believe her. The perpetrator was a neighbour and the response of the mother was, "How could he have done this to me?" The little girl was extremely hurt and very confused. The mother hadn't been assaulted–the child was. Trust that is shattered at such a young age is extremely difficult, if not impossible, to mend. Not surprisingly that child, now grown, finds it very difficult to trust people. She made judgements of her mother (who did not believe her), her father (who did nothing to defend her even though he was not present) and also of God. When we asked her to go back to that day as a little girl and see where Jesus was in the situation her first response was "Jesus wasn't there at all". "But Jesus said He would never leave you nor forsake you so He must have been there." "OK. But He is just standing there. Why doesn't He stop him. I was just a little girl!" "But you see, Jesus didn't come to <u>prevent</u> sin, but to forgive sin. If He was to stop all the bad things from happening we would not have free will." Jesus can redeem situations and bring good from them. Not always immediately and usually not the way we would like. But this lady was still not satisfied. "What good did Jesus bring from this?" "You were not killed were you?" Suddenly the whole situation took on a different face. She still has a great deal more work to do to be able to trust Jesus in an intimate relationship but a good start has been made.

Old hurts and wounds play a huge part in preventing us from entering into a healthy relationship with our Bridegroom. Many times, especially if we have been travelling this road for any length of time, we will not even realize that there are old wounds that need to be revisited. This happened to me one fall over a period of a few months.

At the end of that September my last surviving aunt on my dad's side graduated to be with the Lord. I went with my brother and sister-in-law to the funeral in Chilliwack. They live in Ladysmith, a few miles north of Victoria, so I stayed with them the night before we caught the ferry to the Mainland extremely early the next morning. It was a bright sunny beautiful autumn day–as good a day for an afternoon funeral as any and much better than rain. There were many cousins who had gathered as Aunty Jo was one of our favourites. One of her daughters had come from Australia so it was a time of catching up on everybody's families and activities. After a very long day we left to go home and my brother decided to go by way of a different ferry. On the way he decided to take a short detour–to the cemetery where our mother who died in 1955, is buried. He didn't ask me if I would like to do that. He just did it.

It had been more than 50 years since I had visited her grave and after the long and emotional day I was quite unprepared for what happened. My brother and sister-in-law left me by myself for awhile. I stood beside her grave and looked at the sky and just shouted, "Why? Why did You bring me here? Why did I have to come here today of all days? I've dealt with all this stuff so many times! Why?" And the tears pouring down my face put the lie to that last statement. I fell to my knees on the grass and just bawled. And the Lord was silent. Totally, maddeningly, silent! Eventually I wiped my face and we continued to the ferry.

At the beginning of that November, I went with my friends Jan, Bonnie, Mary and Elissa to a Ladies Retreat that coincidentally was also held in Chilliwack. At the Saturday morning session the speaker was teaching about the importance of receiving storgé love–the kind of mother love that enables a child to develop into a secure personality, able to enter the world with confidence. I don't remember a whole lot of what else she might have said because I just found myself (in the spirit) crying again beside my mother's grave. This time the Lord was with me and He began to explain that all the things in my life that I have regarded as failures, disappointments, lost dreams and hopes, broken relationships and the list goes on and on, were really the Lord not allowing me to be taken in a direction that would lead away from the destiny He had planned for me. He asked me to agree and to give Him permission to change any of my plans that do not lead to His destiny for me.

It has taken me a little while but I realize that I have been given a choice. I can rejoice in Father's loving care and protection that I recognize in hindsight. Or I can continue my learned and habitual response of refusing to hope, shutting down dreams, and hiding behind previous failures so I don't try anything new. I am full of amazement at women who travel the world by themselves. My timid self hides at the very thought of such an adventure. Can I trust my Father, my Friend Jesus and the never failing presence of the Holy Spirit to really venture into the destiny God has planned for me?

If I look at this through the 'ezer knegdo' lens, the first things I must do is to identify the enemy and his tactics. The enemy is always Satan and this time intimidation, fear (of the unknown, failure and others), and shame are his arrows of choice. When God created Eve and gave her the same mandate as Adam, the task was to keep, protect, guard and tend His garden. It did not involve weeding but warfare! Following the Fall the Lord God promised that there would come a time when there would be a rematch between Satan and Adam and Eve. It will not just be Adam versus Satan but Eve will have to participate as well for it to be a genuine rematch. So Eve's daughters have a very steep learning curve ahead of them. This is no time to be timid and uninvolved. Now is the time to learn how to truly be the 'helper' Father God originally designed me and other women to be. That rematch time is getting close.

I pray that the Holy Spirit will teach me how to dream again, how to hope and lay hold of the destiny that was always part of God's plan for my life. Teach me Lord, the strategies I need to develop, to be able to work with Paul and others to defeat Satan's tactics and to build Your kingdom on earth as it is in heaven. It is time to prepare.

Chapter 8

BECOMING GOD'S FRIEND

I wonder what the disciples thought when Jesus said, in John 15:15, "I no longer call you servants, because a servant does not know his master's business. I have called you friends, for everything that I learned from my Father I have made known to you." Had they been thinking of themselves as servants or did they think they were already His friends? I suspect that they were a bit bewildered when He said that He had made known everything He had learned from His Father because there were still so many unanswered questions in their minds. The next few days would surely have proven that they really hadn't learned very much about His Father's business at all. As well as feeling sad at His words that He was going away I suspect that there was some confusion too. Can you hear them thinking–even saying in whispers–"Jesus we've always gone with You everywhere. Why can't we come with You this time? Where are You going that we can't come too? If we're Your friends please take us with You."

How does one make 'friends' with Jesus? In that same John 15 passage Jesus says "You did not choose Me but I chose you...." so just like every other friendship we have, it begins by choosing to get to know one another, do things together and develop intimacy with one another. Intimacy with Jesus reaches into the heart of God and comes from sharing life together.

There are no formulas for becoming Jesus' friends but there are clues. Let's start with, "Do not be anxious about anything, but in everything, by prayer and petition, with thanksgiving, present your request to God." (Phil 4: 6-7) Those are just 20 simple words but when you are in the middle of a muddle, getting the anxiety to quieten down enough to be able to express your thoughts, much less listen for God's voice, is extremely difficult. I've been in some muddles–and known the anxiety–but not been able to put that scripture into practice. I know all of you can also think of your own muddling situations. Often, for me, money is involved.

When we were building our house, quite a few years ago now, the interest rates on the building mortgage kept going up and up and up. It started at 13.5%–which was high enough already–but was 19 ¾% before we were finished building six months later. All the cost estimates came in way over budget–sometimes many thousands of dollars over. We had counted on being able to sell our house in town and paying for the new house entirely from the proceeds of our old house. We were going to do it all <u>for</u> Jesus, like He needed our help. When all was said and done we were still in debt about $125,000.00 and the interest rate went up shortly after to 22 ¼%. I cried a lot! Our daughter Heather, who was all of 10 years old at the time, said to me one day, "Well God never said things were going to be easy." That didn't make me feel any better.

Then the Lord spoke to me in a dream which, in part, was meeting Him in a large hall (which I somehow knew was in heaven) and He was dressed in a business suit. He handed me a balance sheet which

I knew from having worked in a bank needed to have the credits and debits equal in order to be balanced. We understood from that dream that Jesus was our business partner and He would make sure that things were covered. That is exactly what happened but it didn't mean that I was totally free of anxiety for the next few months while all the details were worked out. I was just learning that I could truly trust Jesus in all things. We were certainly thankful and expressed our thanks many times and in many ways. However we did not yet understand all the long term intentions of the Lord. For years after, we were very reluctant to spend money though we always faithfully gave our tithe. We pinched pennies, made do with what we already had and denied ourselves and our kids extras that could have made life easier. We did not want to get into a financial mess again.

Quite a few years later, in 1990, Paul was injured in a vehicle accident and was unable to continue working. This time, though we prayed constantly for healing, wisdom, understanding, finances and many other issues, we still did not understand that Jesus was still our 'business partner' even though He had told us so much earlier, that the 'business' was called 'God And Sons Unlimited'. Again finances were a big part of my anxiety at the time of the accident because we still had kids at home and their needs were much bigger than they had been earlier. Jennifer was at university, Heather was in nurses training and engaged to be married and Peter was in High School. Paul was greatly incapacitated in that he barely spoke and I couldn't discuss much with him. Finances were a total mystery for him at that time. It was a desperate, lonely and extremely anxious time. I got part of the scripture right. I certainly prayed, petitioned and gave thanks that Paul had not been killed as I presented everything to God. But I failed to understand that I could utterly trust God with my total situation so I didn't need to be anxious about anything. Things got to the point that we had just $100.00 in our bank account before there started to be some relief financially. Even then I didn't see it as having been the Lord's resolution to the situation. I credited the Insurance Company.

One autumn I attended a Ladies Retreat in November with a couple of friends. I had heard the lady who was the speaker before and from the experiences she shared it was so obvious that she really knew how to be Jesus' friend and therefore she could go through some of the amazing experiences she did without a single trace of anxiety. I set about to find out how to do that too.

It is very easy to say that it is all based in loving trust. Trust is something that has to grow. It is not automatic and it takes lots of practice and relationship-building activities. Think about trapeze artists in a circus. They have to have absolute trust in one another in order to let go of that swing and know for certain that their partner will catch them every time. They practice for many hours every day. Do I trust Jesus everyday? Truly trust Him with my life and not just my head knowledge? Or do I depend on my own abilities (which were a gift from Him in the first place)? Is my faith really faith or just wishful hoping? More to the point can Jesus trust me?

One of the things that the speaker, Isobel Allum, shared with us was that when she has a problem that is causing her some concern she calls for a 'business meeting' with the Lord. She was a business woman before getting into full time ministry so that seemed natural for her. She would set a time, get dressed into business clothes and meet with Jesus at an appointed time. I shared this concept with Paul after the Retreat so we arranged to have a business meeting with

Jesus too. After all Jesus had said many years before that He was our business partner.

We agreed to meet with Jesus at 11 am one Tuesday. We got dressed into clothes such as we would wear if we were going to meet our banker. We had an agenda, read in the form of a 'talking' prayer, the minutes of previous 'business' transactions/meetings were spoken like remembering many previous experiences with the Lord, which also sort of acted like the Old Business part of a formal meeting. Then we laid out the New Business that we wanted to bring to our Senior Partner's attention, namely the disastrous state of our relationships with our children and loans that we gave them, unquestionably unwisely in retrospect.

I am learning that business partners deal with a great deal more than just finances. I have to confess that in my limited thinking I was regarding 'redemption'–Jesus is my Redeemer–as rescue–He will bail me out of my mistakes. I was not doing that very consciously. I really had not thought the whole thing through properly. I suspect– no, I know–that that is why the Lord continues to allow me to get into situations that I can't handle on my own and I need to cry out to Him for help. Redemption, I am learning, means so much more than Jesus just filling in the gaps where my abilities are inadequate. It is as if we've gone to a restaurant for lunch and the bill comes to $50.00 but I only have $40.00 in my purse. Jesus doesn't just pull out His wallet and cover the $10.00 I'm missing. He knows ahead of time what is in my wallet and suggests He take us to the Empress Hotel instead! Redemption with Jesus always comes with a huge upgrade.

Especially here, in this very secular culture, we have such an independent way of thinking, we don't fully understand that Jesus doesn't just tag along with us to fix our mess-ups. He wants us to work with Him to establish His kingdom. When He said "Seek <u>first</u> the Kingdom of heaven and all these things will be added to you" He really meant it. If I am not absolutely convinced that His love for me is totally unconditional and without measure then I <u>will</u> get anxious about a mortgage, unruly children, an injured husband and everything else that the enemy of my soul will try to use to convince me that my faithful Father in heaven has not called me to be His friend. Jesus said in Matt 11:29, "Take My yoke upon you and I will give you rest." I confess that I usually translate that as 'Jesus would You please come and take one side of <u>my</u> yoke?'

Redemption also includes Jesus sharing His hopes and dreams with us. He wants to build a kingdom on earth as it is in heaven. He wants us to be part of that building process. That is part of the redemption of the world. It is so much more than paying the mortgage. I talked earlier about harvest time on the prairies where I was born. The ability of the pioneers to work together wasn't just at harvest. If a barn needed to be built or one burned down, the men would gather together and have a new one built in just a day or two. Their cows and horses were essential for survival and especially if it was winter, could not be left outside at minus 30 degrees. Have you ever wondered where the word 'fellowship' came from? It is an Anglo-Saxon word that was used to describe the habit the peasants had of herding and pasturing their animals together. Their animals represented their wealth and they had to really trust one another to pasture their wealth together.

In a pioneering community such as was the early beginning of this nation, if a new school was needed the people would appoint a time and pool their resources, go to town, buy the needed supplies and get the thing built. They were friends out of need and learned to work together to get the job done. It was really no different in Jesus' day. He met Peter, James, John and Andrew when they were mending their fishing nets together after working hard all night. It was what friends do. So now when Jesus said He calls us His friends we need to regard that as a call from the King who loves us and knows each of us by name to participate in building His kingdom on earth as it is in heaven according to His blueprint.

Another aspect of being friends with Jesus is that He will confide in you. I have had a couple of experiences that have just delighted my spirit immensely. I received a phone call one day at about lunch time with a text message. Now I do not own a cell phone so this was most unusual. The message said, "Please continue to pray for me. I'll call later". It also told me the cell number of the caller which I did not recognize. So I called the number and just got an answering machine which told me a name. I have a friend by that name so all afternoon I prayed for her, mostly in tongues. By 4:30 I still had not heard back from her so I called her at home. She was very surprised. She had not called me but she definitely needed prayer. The message that called me said it was from Rogers Wireless. My friend said she used to use Rogers but switched to Bell about three years ago. My friend was so encouraged that the Lord had arranged for someone to pray for her when she really needed it even though she herself had not asked directly. We never did figure out the mystery but since I had been praying in tongues certainly my friend was blessed and perhaps even the person who had misdirected the call in the first place had her needs met by our great multi-tasking Redeemer. By the way this is another example of what the Nicean Creed calls 'the communion of saints'.

The second incident was when we were visiting with our friend Dave Richardson one afternoon during his visit to Victoria. In the middle of our conversation suddenly I felt the Lord say that when Dave and his wife Lesley got back to Jerusalem they would find that a tree in their garden would be sprouting new leaves unexpectedly. That seemed like a weird sort of message but I decided to speak it anyway....and if I seemed weird well so what? I got an email about a week later saying that while they were away a gardener had cut down some trees but one of them was putting out a sprout that showed promise of growing into a tree again. The Lord had indicated to me that this would be an assurance to them that a new ministry they were starting was something that He was pleased with. I was so excited that Jesus had confided that to me and given me the opportunity to share it to encourage Dave and Lesley.

One year I decided to systematically read through the whole Bible–something I had never done before. Oh, I've got lots of favourite stories, verses and passages but I had never read the whole thing systematically from Genesis to Revelation. One of the things that really became obvious is that there are a great many instructions about food, especially in Leviticus. Over and over the same instructions are repeated about where the sacrifices are to be made, the time of day, who is to participate, where the fat is to be burned, where the hides and offal are to be disposed of and by whom. It becomes very tedious reading and I asked the Lord why He felt He needed to repeat things so often. There are sin offerings, wave offerings, daily sacrifices and the lists go on and on. It always seemed to involve food and blood and I wondered why. The response I feel the Lord gave me was very intriguing. I felt He was saying that there needed to be a constant daily reminder to the people that He, the Lord Himself, was a very present part of their community and just as they would have to feed the father of the family or the children, or the mother, the Lord's Presence also needed to be fed as a very valued member of the family. We have seen in our own culture how easy it is to leave the Lord out of our thinking, planning, and family life so very possibly the Lord knew that that could happen to His Jewish people too and made regulations to try to avoid that calamity.

The other thing that was repeated over and over was the Lord's assurances that He would go before them, He would defeat their enemies, He would show them the way to take in the wilderness, He would never leave them because He loved them with an ever lasting love. I lost track of the number of times He emphasized His constant Presence with them. Reading it as a whole instead of bits and bites here and there gave quite a different picture than I had before.

Things are becoming clearer for me now. It is very much like falling in love. When Paul was courting me he was offering me a very different way of living than what I had had up until then. I was a city girl. He was very comfortable in both city and country, especially the forest. He made all sorts of rash(?) promises such as he would always buy me flowers when he took me out to dinner. It is perhaps a good thing for our bank account that he has not remembered that promise as I think I really prefer his spontaneous suggestions for dinner out now and then.

I am coming to understand that my friendship with Jesus also means that, like my pioneer forebears who knew the joys of the many helps of friends, this is a Friendship I can absolutely depend on for everything in life. This is friendship on a totally different scale. To paraphrase Graham Cooke, this is an unparalleled, upgraded understanding of friendship. Jesus says He chose me to be His friend (John

15:16) and that He loves me with an everlasting love (Jer 31:3). He promises that all His plans for me are for good and not for evil to bring me to an expected hope and a future. (Jer 29:11) So where does that put all the anxiety about mortgages, money and accidents? Right under the Lord's feet! It also includes the rebellious children I love. In John 14: 13-14 Jesus assures His grieving disciples that "...anyone who has faith in Me may ask for anything in My Name and He will do it because He is in the Father and the Father is in Him." So Lord I ask for the salvation of all my children and grandchildren. Isa 49:25-26 declares most emphatically, "Can plunder be taken from warriors, or captives rescued from the fierce? But this is what the Lord says; Yes captives will be taken from warriors, and plunder retrieved from the fierce; I will contend with those who contend with you, and your children I will save. " "Is anything too difficult for God (Gen 18:14)?" Those worries all just become the enemy's tricks to make me stumble, that Jesus promises "to defeat and sweep away before me". (Deut 9:3). "I will never leave you as orphans". (John 14:18). "I have placed before you an open door that no one can shut". (Rev. 3:8). "If anyone loves Me, he will obey My teaching. My Father will love him (her), and we will come to him and make our home with him." (John 14:23)

All of this to say that the Lord is now emphasizing His desire to be understood not only as Saviour, as Redeemer, as Lord but most lovingly as Friend inferring close personal friendship that wants to be involved in all aspects of our lives. Increase that desire in our hearts too, precious Lord and Friend.

Chapter 9
PREPARING FOR A WEDDING

A number of years ago now I remember reading an article in the Readers Digest about a series of advertisements that were placed on the sides of buses in a city in the U.S. They said things like: "That 'Love Your Neighbour Thing'–I really meant it! Signed Jesus". "Have you read My #1 best seller? There will be a test! Signed God". "We need to talk. Signed God". "What part of 'Thou shalt not' did you not understand? signed God". The one that really caught my eye was : "Loved the wedding. Invite Me to the marriage. signed Jesus".

In our culture we have built a huge multi million dollar industry around the whole wedding event with special planners, rental services for everything from clothes to glassware, flowers, music, food, even special chapels that do nothing else but perform weddings. The trappings have become so extensive and expensive that for far too many people the real significance of the commitment is never addressed. A few years ago I heard a story about a woman in California who was so desperate to have a wedding that she actually organized a huge affair with hundreds of guests and the white dress and all so that she could marry herself! Perhaps she reasoned that since about half of all marriages end in divorce she would just dispense with the groom bit and save herself some money in the long run but still have a good party. God's purposes for marriage have not just been trivialized but, to our peril, have been totally aborted from God's original vision.

Many of us in the church have heard about the Bride of Christ. Most of us have some concept of being called to be that Bride. Some of us even wonder about how the 'One New Man'–the reconciliation of Jews and Christians–fits into the picture of the Messiah's Bride. There is no suggestion that there will be two brides–one Jewish and one Christian–so that suggests that at some point there will be a coming together into one flock with one Shepherd. Usually discussions in a Christian context about being the Bride include apologies to the men who have trouble visualizing themselves in a dress. Women have no less difficulty, it seems at times, with being 'sons' of God. Perhaps because we have concentrated for far too long on the outward trappings of a wedding we have lost sight of the much more important spiritual aspects of a marriage.

When Paul and I were married more than 50 years ago the sum total of any spiritual marriage preparation consisted of our pastor meeting with us once to discuss the ceremony and give us a bit of advice. He said that about 90% of all couples who have been married more than three years find that any real conversation amounts to about two minutes a day. Most discussions and/or arguments are about money. Before our wedding day one of my aunts quietly took me aside and advised me to get my doctor to prescribe birth control pills which were actually quite new at that time. There was absolutely no mention of spiritual preparation for our marriage. Not even a suggestion that our marriage should be a reflection of the Lord's relationship with His coming marriage to His Bride. Our lives were very full of all sorts of other concerns. Paul was busy preparing for university exams. I concentrated on making dresses, arranging for flowers, pictures, invitations and organizing a reception. The one thing we did do–though not because it was advised by any of our spiritual mentors–was to be baptized together by total immersion two weeks before our wedding. It was not until many years later that we came to an understanding of how extremely significant that event was in how we developed spiritually. We suspect that that decision was something the Holy Spirit arranged since He is the very best marriage counsellor there could possibly be.

We can be very certain that the Holy Spirit will make sure that the Beloved Bride is properly prepared for her perfect marriage with the Messiah. If we understand some of the Jewish traditions surrounding marriage we will be better able to appreciate more of what the Bible tells us and be able to co-operate with the Holy Spirit as He leads those preparations. When we understand the Jewish customs and language that accompanies a wedding, a beautiful new music emerges from the words that we have not really recognized. I am very grateful that my friend Janet has taught me about some of the details of a Jewish betrothal as, in our Western thinking, we have missed some very important understandings about the process. Essentially we have a very Hellenistic/secular worldview in Western society that prevents us from recognizing, understanding and appreciating our Jewish roots.

Unlike our very modern young people who think it is perfectly all right to live together before they are married, Orthodox Jewish couples are very circumspect during their courtship. When Janet and I were in Jerusalem in 2007 we saw young couples sitting together in hotel lobbies–a very public place–and discreetly talking with one another, perhaps sharing a soft drink or even a glass of water. One evening we watched as two fathers and a rabbi joined one of the young couples and much earnest discussion took place. It seemed that they were planning a marriage not just a wedding.

The following excerpted material is shared to fill some of the deficiencies in our Western understanding.

To begin the process of understanding we need to take a short journey through the ancient Jewish betrothal process. In a beautiful way we will see who Yeshua, Jesus our Messiah and saviour is, and how much this relates to your own identity and value to Yeshua and the Father. It affects how you both receive and give love to Him.

Our hearts were designed to receive God's love and to love Him in return. He has always wanted a bride for His son. The male and female of God were placed in man at creation but became separated by God so there could be reciprocal love between Adam and Eve. We had a oneness with Jesus and the Father before the fall in the garden—that is what He has always wanted to restore.

*Betrothal–is also called **kiddushim**–meaning sanctified or set apart. It is a very rich and full period of time that sets the foundation for marriage. It was customary for the groom's father to select a bride for his son, but often the son might let his father know that there was a certain young woman that he wished to have as his bride. The groom's father would then contact the bride's father and invite the prospective bride to a meal at the groom's home. It would be a wonderfully sumptuous meal filled with delicacies to impress the girl! The father, son and hoped-for bride would eat this meal together. Remember, a meal is often the place where a covenant is made.*

*After eating, a wedding contract or **Ketubah** is presented to the girl. Ketubah means 'written' in Hebrew. In this document, the groom* *would make promises to his bride; he offers a lot to show how much worth she has to him, and these are not empty promises. These are legal obligations; if she accepts these promises, she gets the scroll– it is hers and it has powerful legal rights she can call into account even in court at a later date.*

*If she accepts, then a **Mohar** or purchase price is set and it represents a value–a rich family would be able to offer more than a more modest one. He is not 'buying' her per se, he is attributing value by giving up something of himself. Adam gave up part of himself to have Eve. In another sense, the mohar frees her from her father's household. (Gen 24:53)*

*Now we come to the most important part of this ceremony. The father pours a cup of wine and the son drinks from it and passes it to the bride. **It is called the "cup of acceptance"**. Everything in the betrothal process hinges on her drinking from it. When she receives it and drinks she is betrothed–she has entered a covenant relationship. (see Matt 26:27) If she does not drink there is no wedding. In this process the bride always had the right of refusal.*

*When she accepts and drinks from the cup, this exchange of drinking is called **"the kiss in the cup"**. The bridegroom has left a little part of himself on the lip of the cup, and a little part of him goes into her. They are now legally betrothed and legally bound together. They would need to go to court to get a divorce if this agreement is broken even before the marriage is consummated. This is where Joseph and Mary were when Joseph found out that Mary was expecting a baby. Initially he intended to go through the legal part of a divorce very quietly to protect her, until he had a revelation about who the child was.*

After all this excitement comes a time of parting when the bride returns to her house and the groom to his father's house. This would be a period of about a year during which the groom would prepare new living quarters for his bride by adding on to his father's house. He would focus particularly on creating a beautiful bridal chamber that would be a much better place than where the bride is coming from. (John 14: 1-4)

*Before this parting the young man would make an **oath**, usually to give up wine until they were married–he would be giving up something important and pleasurable. (Matt 26:29) Also he would give her gifts to remind her of his love and commitment during the long separation ahead. (Eph 4:8)*

*MEANWHILE, the bride is also focused on her own preparations with the help and excitement of her friends. She enters a **mikveh**, a special ritual bath of water in which she is totally immersed–fingers spread, eyes open, everything exposed to the water, signifying purification and sanctification. She rises out of the water to put on a new garment and her bridal veil is presented. It is a thick veil, with only her eyes visible signifying she is set apart, reserved for her bridegroom. She will not appear in public without this.*

The exact date of the wedding is kept a secret. It depends on the room being ready and even more importantly, on the father's approval of the bridal chamber and the finances. It is said when the groom would be asked the date, he would say "only my father knows." (Acts 1:7)

Once he got the go ahead, the bridegroom would secretly gather the wedding party. The bride would probably hear something through the grapevine about the imminence and keep herself beautiful and prepared for his secret arrival. That must have been a time of great anticipation.

The wedding party would usually come at night with torches with the best man blowing the shofar and shouting "Behold the bridegroom comes" as they were arriving. It was like a well rehearsed game called "kidnapping the bride". She would be lifted up on a palette-like cart and carried by the groom's friends. (This reminds us of the Ark of the Covenant being lifted up–His shekinah glory rested on the ark.)

Then they came under a **chuppah** *or canopy signifying a new household is being formed. It also represents the tabernacle, the eternal dwelling place of God. There is a Jewish belief that God hovers over the chuppah and that He is never closer than during this ceremony. The bride walks around the bridegroom seven times. This is very significant. Remember Jericho when the walls came down?–seven times means there will be no walls in the relationship. It also gives the groom the opportunity to admire his beloved from all angles! We have also learned that the Hebrew word for helper (called helpmeet in our English bibles) is 'ezer'–one who walks around and sets the boundaries. Women have been given this power to set the context of the relationship.*

Vows are then said and the bride and groom go into the bridal chamber for seven days. It is a place of beauty and intimacy–beautiful tapestries, candles, food and wine as well as tempting delicacies. After the seven days they come out to celebrate the Marriage Supper with all their friends and family.

Scripture is full of wedding and marriage images. In Hosea 2:19 God said to Israel: I will betroth you to me forever. I will betroth you in righteousness and justice, in love and compassion. I will betroth you in faithfulness and you will acknowledge the Lord. When John baptized Jesus, the words spoken over him were a Messianic title– "This is my Son, the Beloved." (Matt 3:17)

This is the Messiah they were expecting. In John 3:29 John the Baptizer also clarified that he was not the Messiah by pointing out that "the bridegroom is the one who has the bride". So interesting that he referred to Yeshua as the bridegroom, knowing that his description was one that the people around him understood in reference to the Messiah. Yeshua himself also referred to himself as a bridegroom in Luke 5:35.

A short pause is needed in order to emphasise some points in what we have just learned. It amazes me constantly that we can read things in our Bibles many times and fail to grasp the significance of the words. This is at least one reason, I think, why it is important to read more than one version of scripture. I'm convinced that there are times when a little spirit comes in the middle of the night and rewrites words, sentences and even whole paragraphs in my Bible while I sleep.

One afternoon I was reading a book written by a Messianic Jewish lady named Sandra Templinski. She wrote a simple little statement that 'we need to understand the Ten Commandments differently. From a Hebraic point of view they are <u>a ketuba</u>–a marriage contract or betrothal. She went on to say that when Jesus delivered His message that we call the Sermon on the Mount, He was expanding on the Ten Commandments. I had never made that connection before but when I looked more closely I gained a great deal of understanding.

We need to understand the circumstances when the original Commandments were given in Deuteronomy 5: 6-21. When the former Hebrew slaves stood before the flaming mountain at Sinai,

God was reinforcing through Moses the marriage contract with this nation that God had chosen to be His Bride forever. The encounter with God at Mount Sinai was overwhelming. The people ran away in terror from this living God who spoke to them in audible words that they could understand. God was offering them a relationship based on His love for them, not on a religion based on rules. But their slave mentality prevented them from realizing the full import of such a marriage. Because of their fear and lack of understanding they then wandered in the wilderness for forty years, learning the hard way to obey His words and trust His commandments and statutes. In the process they had to fight wars, map out strategies for wilderness survival and develop co-operative relationships with one another. They passed test after test, and developed from a company of ex-slaves to a nation that could fight together to enter the Promised Land .

Going back to Deuteronomy 5, in verses 6–7 God says (according to Shirley paraphrase) "I have chosen this nation to be My Bride and you will have no other husband." In verses 8–10 He reminds them that the kind of false gods that they had been used to when they were slaves in Egypt are now 'out of bounds'. There would be no extra marital spiritual affairs amongst His people. Even further, there are consequences for wandering away and rewards for faithfulness. I have always understood verse 11 to mean that we should not swear using God's name–which is never a good idea anyway–but I think there is much more implied here. For the Jews, names are extremely important and carry great meaning. Time and time again God identified Himself to His people by revealing one of His names that declared one of His attributes. Such revelations revealed His character, intentions and power as well as His great desire for fellowship with us. I'm going to come back to this idea more fully later.

In verses 12–15, by establishing Sabbath rest God is not putting onerous restrictions on His people as has so often been interpreted. As I was pondering all of this in terms of being married to Him I realized what God's heart was saying by commanding that the Sabbath be kept holy. He knew by His own design that people were not meant to work constantly but needed a break on every seventh day at the very least. It became a legalistic thing full of silly rules about not carrying a needle in a lapel, not walking more than a prescribed distance, not pushing elevator buttons or using tools or equipment. What God was really wanting was a guaranteed "date night/day" every week with the Bride He loves passionately! He wanted a time to laugh with us, to go for a walk in His fabulous creation, to admire our efforts to utilize the creativity He has deposited within each of us, to get us to enjoy His company like lovers should. That should be a treat.

The whole issue of honouring parents (verse 16) is not well understood in our culture today. It is really about establishing boundaries in very close family relationships. Early in Genesis we are told that a man will leave his father and mother (Gen 2:24) and cleave to his wife but think about the reality of that statement. The new couple didn't move to a different town or to a different street. They set up a new tent on the other side of the communal fire perhaps, or, in later times, built a new room on the family home. Though they lived in close proximity there were boundaries established between generations that were based on mutual respect for changing needs in the development of relationships. When they are young, children have few responsibilities and easy access to their parents but there comes a time when there is a need to enable maturity that is built on respect to develop co-operative community relationships. Child-care was also part of the plan since it really is true that it takes a village or extended family to raise a child. Protection from enemies and wild animals, production of food, and the preservation of language, history and culture depends on proper honouring of the older generation. When God declared Himself to be the God of Abraham, Isaac and Jacob, the lesson that we are meant to learn is that our communities are to be based on family generations working together harmoniously. Our Western culture is excessively individualistic and fractured for the most part, for this commandment to be appreciated. However in this fifth commandment God is promising that blessings of peace and prosperity are attached to the honouring of parents. Personally, I think that such honouring extends to honouring the Jews as the fathers of our faith and the English as the fathers of our governmental system as well.

If the first five commandments are about our relationship with God the next five commandments are the 'great THOU SHALT NOTS' which are designed to keep our interpersonal relationships righteous. Perhaps because they are written as negatives they tend to give a sense of negativity to all the commandments. However, if you turn them around and write them as positives you get a very different view that makes a lot more sense.

So "Thou shalt not murder" becomes "Bring life and honour it!" "Thou shalt not commit adultery" becomes "Guard with great integrity and faithfulness the marriage bond". "Thou shalt not steal" becomes "Be aware of the needs of your fellow citizens and be generous". "Thou shalt not give false testimony against your neighbour" becomes "Guard truth and use it to protect your neighbour". "Thou shalt not covet your neighbour's wife. You shall not set your desire on your neighbour's house or land, his manservant or maidservant, his ox or donkeys or anything that belongs to your neighbour" becomes "Be content with what the Lord your God has given you in every respect".

Now at this point in my reading and reflections something happened in my spirit that I had not been expecting. The more I prayed about these things, the more I started to see and appreciate the yearning heart of love that our God wants to pour all over us. Suddenly "God" was no longer distant and rather impersonal. Suddenly He was very present, very gentle, with tender, loving concern for the greatest happiness, joy, health, welfare, prosperity, hope, faith and love for this magnificent creation that He has always intended to be spectacularly, overwhelmingly, beautiful. There are just no words to describe the little glimpse He opened for me. It was so much more than just recognizing Him as Father! All I could do was just be silent and weep.

I also caught a little inkling of the ache in His heart at how much we have misunderstood Him. As I found a new way of relating to Papa I longed to be able to comfort Him and assure Him that I had seen a new side of His love, that was not just for me but for all His people also. Perhaps I am just speaking for myself but in my thinking He has been rather stern, distant and very hard to reach and please. It is very hard to have a vital relationship with Someone you can't see, touch or clearly hear. Perhaps because my own Dad tended not to be very involved with us kids before our Mum died, my view of my heavenly Father was rather distorted. The middle part of the last century was very unkind to fathers as they tried to cope with all the destructive forces unleashed against men as a result of many wars that took them away from their families for long periods of time.

Then I turned to Matthew chapters 5–7. The words are very familiar to us, but have you ever noticed verse 21 of chapter 5? "You have heard that it was said to the people long ago "Do not murder" and anyone who murders will be subject to judgement. But I tell you that anyone who is angry with his brother will be subject to judgement." How easy is it to be angry? Have I ever thought of anger as 'murder'? I know only too well that there have been times when my anger has exploded and I have hurt people I love, but I would never have labelled myself as a murderer. Or how about chapter 6: 22? "The eye is the lamp of the body. If your eyes are good, your whole body will be full of light. But if your eyes are bad your whole body will be full of darkness." We learned in David Stern's Jewish New Testament that those words are actually a colloquial expression meaning that we are to be generous in all our relationships and bad eyes indicate stinginess. Does that sound like the new understanding the Lord gave me for "Thou shalt not steal"? When Jesus spoke verses 19 to 21 of that chapter about storing up treasures in heaven because where your treasure is, there your heart will be also, did His hearers that day so long ago, equate it with "Do not covet"? In so many ways all through the New Testament Jesus indicated that our final destination is a real place called 'heaven' and it is His joy to make sure we get there.

I want to look at John 14 for a few minutes. Jesus is having a final Seder meal with His best friends and He reveals to them what is going to happen next. Bob Jones claimed that Jesus doesn't keep secrets from us and this is a fine example. Jesus knows only too well what is about to happen but He puts the information into terms that His Jewish disciples understand as betrothal language. At the beginning of their three and a half years with Him they heard John the Baptiser say clearly that he, John, was not the Messiah but was the 'friend of the Bridegroom'. He proclaimed, "Behold the Lamb of God who takes away the sin of the world." Now Jesus is saying to

His disciples that He is going away to build a room on His Father's house to prepare for His Bride to come to live after their marriage. Very straightforward betrothal language that they, as Jews, would all have understood but which we, for the most part, miss since so much of the Jewishness has been eliminated from our Bibles. I'm going to borrow a bit more from what was shared earlier to really round out our understanding of the Betrothal.

*During the Last Supper Yeshua offers a **ketuba**–a covenant with many promises. "I will never leave you. I will come back for you. I am going to make a place for you. You can ask anything in my name." He had already promised centuries earlier in Jeremiah 31:31 that he would make a new covenant with the house of Israel–a covenant into which we are now grafted. He would put the law within them, and they would be taught who God is–each person would know him intimately for him or herself.*

*The **mohar** or price he was willing to pay was very clearly stated. "This is my body and my blood given for you." He was giving his life as the mohar. We are bought by the blood of the Lamb, bought to know his love completely with no barriers. We will know him directly now with no walls between us, no walls between us and the Father and the Son.*

*Remember the **"kiss in the cup"**–the Cup of Acceptance–whereby the acceptance of the covenant is made? Jesus said "Drink all of it". He wanted them to fully take in his love, his kiss. Yeshua made this covenant, even though he knew the bride would be unfaithful. He still submitted to the will of His Father.*

*At the end of the meal comes ' **the parting**' . Jesus said that He would be going away but that the Holy Spirit would come to give gifts to sustain us through the betrothal time and to reveal to us all truth.*

*Then He took the **oath**. "I will not drink of the fruit of the vine until I drink it anew in the kingdom." He is waiting for the marriage banquet with us. Satan tried to get Him to drink wine on the cross to break his oath, but Jesus refused. He is completely faithful to His bride. (Mark 15:23)*

When we take the cup, His blood given for us, we are taking the cup of acceptance. We become one with Him; bound together in a love covenant. We went to the cross with Him–this is the power of covenant. Our sin and separation from the Father was taken care of there. We came alive in Him when His body was once again made alive. Everything He did was a reversal of what was lost in the garden.

And the spikenard that Mary poured out on Him? He did not smell death on the cross. He was so completely saturated with the nard that the fragrance on him was the fragrance of us–His bride. We were there with Him and a reminder of the joy that was set before Him for which he endured all things.

Remember, you are set apart, you are cherished, you have been given a beautiful ketuba and have been called under the canopy of living with Him. As you take the cup at communion, you are celebrating Him. You are affirming your covenant with Him. You receive His kiss each time you receive this cup.

What are we to understand as we prepare to be the Bride of Christ? Are we aware of being courted by Yeshua? What are our expectations and dreams; what can we expect life to be like as the Bride of the King of Kings? So much of our thinking, praying and planning is based on our individuality that we rarely think what it might be like to be the corporate Nation-Bride. I can be absolutely certain that it will not be like the Borg in Star Wars. We won't be a mass of totally integrated beings that are unable to think as an individual but what will it be like?

Let's suppose for a minute that we (individually at the moment) are that young woman betrothed to a man in our village. For a whole year we don't see one another officially nor speak to each other. But we can't help noticing that the new room on his father's house is progressing. We can't help hearing the rumours. What are we supposed to be looking for as the sign of our imminent wedding?

There have been other times in Israel's history that the people expected 'something' to happen. Daniel was reading the scroll of Jeremiah and realized that the 70 years the prophet had written about was accomplished and it was time to return to Israel. When Mary and Joseph took Jesus to the temple in Jerusalem when He was just eight days old, Simeon "just happened" to be there and exalted the God of his fathers by pronouncing that this Babe–this newborn–was the Messiah. How did Simeon know? What was he looking for? What made the elderly widow Anna proclaim the same thing to all who would listen?

What about us? What are we looking and listening for? Jesus said before He was crucified that the Holy Spirit would tell us of things that were to come and would lead us into all truth. I am hearing many present-day prophets warning that Jesus' return is getting much nearer. We are all hearing about wars and rumours of wars. What are you hearing? What is God saying to you in your prayer times, scripture reading, in circumstances, in dreams and conversations? We will hear the full counsel of our Lord when we listen to what He is saying to each of us. This is partly how we will learn to be a whole Body working together. Not all of us are an eye, not all of us are an ear. Usually the body is so integrated that it is unaware that each part is doing its job because everything works together so smoothly. We are not a Borg but we are called to be the Body of Messiah bringing the Kingdom of heaven to earth, ready for our beloved King.

The material in italics has been excerpted from original teaching presented at Toronto Airport Christian Fellowship in September 2007 by Mark Davidson of Shulamite Ministries. My thanks to Janet Wilson for sharing this material. The original author has given permission to share this material.

Chapter 10
DID I ENLIST OR WAS I DRAFTED?

Psalm 68: 11-14

> The Lord gives the command;
> The women who proclaim the good tidings are a great host:
> Kings of armies flee, they flee,
> And she who remains at home will divide the spoil.
> When you lie down among the sheepfolds,
> You are like the wings of a dove covered with silver,
> And its pinions with glistening gold.
> When the Almighty scattered the kings there,
> It was snowing on Zalmon. NASB

This whole psalm is about war–a women's war really. Several years ago my kids gave me a book for my birthday, written by Ed Silvoso, entitled "Women–God's Secret Weapon". For me this has been an absolutely pivotal book in developing my understanding of who women are in God's grand scheme of things and how I fit into His plans overall. The book focuses on this psalm and unpacks much of the symbolism and the lessons to be learned about God's plans for Eve's daughters.

I was born near the beginning of the Second World War. Some of my earliest memories are of news movies of that war and, as a result, fighting in a war has never been on my "to do list". I don't like conflicts. I hate misunderstandings and divisions. Anger–especially my own–really scares me. So how can I possibly want to be involved in a war for the Lord? I understand spiritual warfare now but you can't imagine how many years I resisted the whole subject. Or the arguments I had with Paul about it! In fact it wasn't until the Lord very graciously showed me a vision about Victoria, my home city, that my point of view changed.

The first part of the vision that I saw was the Lord descending from a cloud and in His hand was a beautiful golden sickle that was very sharp. I could see the light glistening off the edge and I realized that it was a reaping instrument. A few days later I again saw the beginning of the vision but more details were added. The Lord was at the head of a mighty host of angels and saints. All the sky was black with terrific storm clouds forming. The Lord and His host came down the wind of the storm. Jesus was carrying a naked double-edged sword which flashed and glinted in the light. Some of the saints and angels were also armed with swords. Then I could see tiny little men upon the earth, who were hurrying to bring in their crops before the storm broke. They seemed to be aware of the storm but not of the Lord and His host. I noticed that here and there little fires were burning.

A day or so later I again saw the vision–it was sort of like a video that kept being paused. More details were added. There were more little fires burning and it seemed that some people were stumbling about almost in a panic, with what looked like plastic bags over their heads. Some of them fell into the fires that were burning more frequently. Those who fell into a fire seemed to ascend up towards the Lord and His host. Some people got smaller and smaller and then just seemed to twinkle for a second and disappear like when sparks fly up from a fire. Other people got larger and larger until they joined the Lord and His host. I asked the Lord what this was all about, and where the battle would begin, and who the enemy was? He showed me a very busy intersection in downtown Victoria from very high up. I could see that everybody seemed to be in great turmoil bumping into each other, into buildings and wandering into the street. Cars were crashing into each other. I couldn't understand why, so He took me down closer and I saw that everybody looked perfectly normal except for their heads, which were like great blobs of dough. He said to me; "Your enemies are confusion, apathy and ignorance".

With different understanding comes a new way of viewing the world. It is not hard today to see that there is war happening on many fronts. We see shooting wars in Iraq, Afganistan, Israel, Gaza and many other places. We read about the wars on poverty, illiteracy and hunger. It is not hard to identify that there is global war–on terror, in the economies of nations and climate change. Some of these issues are based on reality and some on questionable perceptions. All of them use up resources and energy and cause arguments and dissentions. The "enemies" the Lord told me about–confusion, apathy and ignorance–are evident everywhere.

When we dive under the raging storm of all these wars into the calmer water to find the Lord's perspective in scripture we find a different way of understanding all these conflicts. What is the spirit behind the many wars, the nature of the dissentions and who are the protagonists?

In 1Cor 15:26, it says; "The last enemy to be destroyed is death". In the previous verses in 1 Cor 15, Paul wrote about the Messiah fighting a great battle against evil, destroying all dominion, authority and power and handing the kingdom over to His Father. That sounds to me like the restoration of all things and sends us back to the Garden of Eden again. Genesis 2: 16-17 says; "And the Lord God commanded man; "you are free to eat from any tree in the Garden; but you must not eat from the tree of the knowledge of good and evil, for when you eat of it you will surely die". Then verse 18 follows immediately saying; "The Lord God said, "It is not good for man to be alone. I will make a helper (an ezer knegdo) suitable for him". The Lord then went on to tell Adam to give names to all the creatures the Lord had created but there was no mate found suitable for Adam among all that God had created. That naming exercise was not for God's benefit as though He might have overlooked something but was for Adam's understanding. Adam had to know with certainty that what God was about to do was absolutely the only way things could go. So while Adam snoozed, God brought forth Eve. She was always part of the plan. She had always been within Adam. This was not a case of taking more dust of the earth and creating someone new or even forming a new species. God took a part of Adam, near his heart, and fashioned Eve. When God brought her to Adam he named her 'woman' because she was taken from man. In Hebrew the words are 'Ish' meaning man and 'Ishah' meaning woman. At this point they had not yet sinned. Adam was only continuing to do what God had told him to do–he named her and acknowledged her to be part of himself.

Enter the serpent!!

Why did the serpent, whose more familiar name is Satan or the devil, strike up a conversation with the woman? Adam was right there but it was the woman who was challenged. To be fair, Eve was still within Adam when God gave the instructions about what they could and could not eat. Her answer about the tree in the middle of the garden was not quoted exactly correctly. God had not said that they couldn't touch it, just that if they ate the fruit they would die. Though Adam was right there he remained silent. He could have corrected the conversation but he didn't. Was he waiting to see what might happen to Eve? So the war began. It is not a war between people and God, nor people and Satan. It is a war between God and Satan! We are the targets—the filling in the sandwich in a way—but we're also the prize that God desires with all His heart.

When the Lord God cursed Satan He promised that He would put enmity between Satan and his offspring and the woman's offspring. This enmity is not just hatred. It is implacably, utterly irresolvable separation for all eternity. The Lord was also promising that there would come a Saviour through the woman who would one day make it possible to restore fellowship between God and His people and utterly destroy Satan. The Lord God declared war! God WILL have the last word and He WILL be the victor. In Genesis 3:20 Adam renamed his wife and calls her Eve (Hebrew Havah) which means 'living' because she would become the mother of all the living. So Adam declared Eve's destiny, not just to bear children but to bring forth life.

When the Lord God sent them out of the Garden it was not done in anger but to protect them from the Tree of Everlasting Life. Thus began a process. The Lord did not revoke His original plan to share creation with mankind. The Lord began to prepare a family that then grew into a nation with the task of working and warring with Him, to bring forth His written scriptures to be guarded and handed down from generation to generation. They were to record the history of His relationship with His people to whom He progressively revealed His nature and character. In spite of innumerable mistakes, disobedience and outright sin, God's plans continue to move forward. He has always had a faithful remnant who would listen for His voice.

Generation after generation the daughters of Eve continue to be the main target because Satan has not forgotten that one of her offspring will be his conqueror. (There is a tradition in Islam that the downfall of Islam will come through the women which is why they keep their women under such tight control.) Jewish prophets one after another, repeat the promise of a Saviour. At exactly the right time, Jesus–the Hebrew Yeshua means Yehovah saves–was born to the adoration of angels, shepherds and kings without most people realizing the enormous implications of the event. Satan hasn't stopped hating women but Jesus' birth brings huge changes in the heavenlies for Eve's daughters.

I want to consider two women who were special friends of the Lord while He was here on earth. In Luke 10: 38-42 we meet the sisters Martha and Mary who lived at Bethany. I've heard people say that Jesus was scolding Martha in this passage. Personally I don't believe that. Both the sisters were His friends and I don't think He would do anything that would bring division between them. I think Jesus was reassuring Martha that He didn't want her to wear herself out by trying to do too much. He wanted her to know that she didn't have to earn His friendship and approval. This story is lacking a great deal of detail, like so many other stories in the Bible! I suspect Jesus would have been really pleased if Martha had wanted to be beside

Mary at His feet as well. What did Jesus mean when He said that Mary had "chosen what is better"? What exactly was it that would not be taken from her?

Let's get a closer look at what is happening. Mary is the only woman we are told about who is sitting with all the men hearing what Jesus is teaching. That in itself is most unusual but even more, the Lord is giving her presence His full approval. In Mark 14:7 we read that a woman who is later identified simply as 'Mary' poured extremely expensive perfume on His head to anoint Him. When the disciples rebuked her Jesus corrects them and praises her. It was in the position she desired, sitting at the Lord's feet instead of being in the kitchen, that she alone of all the disciples heard Jesus clearly say that He was going to die. She tuned her heartbeat to His and had the privilege of preparing Him later for what was coming.

In John 11 we learn more about Mary, Martha and their brother Lazarus. Lazarus became very ill and the two sisters sent word to Jesus to urgently come to heal him. In that society Lazarus would have been their only protector and provider. But Jesus delayed for two more days. Then He shocked His disciples by saying that it is time to go back to Bethany to wake Lazarus up. The disciples were confused. Just shortly before, they had all fled from Judea because the Judeans were threatening to kill Jesus. Furthermore, if Lazarus was asleep surely he would recover wouldn't he? Jesus then spoke plainly and explained that Lazarus is dead. Jesus had said that he was asleep. Then He said that he was dead. Jesus was trying to change their understanding of the concept and reality of life and death. He was renaming death and calling it back to life.

When Martha greeted Jesus she declared that her brother would not have died if Jesus had been there. Jesus responded that He

Himself is the resurrection and the life. He asked Martha if she believed that and she declared that she believed that her brother will rise again at the last day and that Jesus is the Messiah. What was her understanding of that title? Was it what we understand and expect? When Mary greeted Jesus she spoke exactly the same words but Jesus' response was quite different. He was moved by compassion at her tears, wept Himself, and went to call Lazarus back to life. What was it about Mary that was so different? Her heartbeat was attuned to His. Mary not only believed in her head but her heart also believed. Know for certain, that Satan is not threatened by any word you don't wholeheartedly believe no matter how many times you repeat it. Remember we said earlier that the last enemy is death. By raising Lazarus, Jesus challenged the religious authorities of the day and declared to Satan that a showdown was imminent.

Earlier I wrote that God didn't just tell Adam and Eve about blood sacrifice but demonstrated it by killing animals to make clothing for them to cover the shame of their sin. Jesus didn't just tell His friends that He had authority over death. He demonstrated it as a fact no less than three times that are recorded in the gospels. The first time was the son of a widow in the town of Nain as recorded in Luke 7:11-17. The second was Jairus' daughter in Capernaum in Luke 8:49-56 where Jesus declared that the child was not dead but asleep. In the case of Lazarus, not only had he been dead for four days but Bethany was also in the vicinity of Jerusalem and this particular miracle was a direct challenge to the religious spirits controlling that territory. Furthermore the priests in Jerusalem were afraid that if they lost control of the people, the Romans would also remove their political power as well. So they planned and plotted. Satan thought that he had the power to bring death but he didn't realize that Jesus had come with the power to overcome death with life.

It was about the time of Passover–the time that celebrates the miracle of life over death for the Jewish people. God's timing is always perfect. Jesus was again visiting with His friends in Bethany where a dinner was given in His honour. Mary took a pint of nard, a very expensive perfume and poured it over His feet wiping them with her hair. She knew He was about to die and she anointed Him. That perfume not only filled the whole house with its scent but would have remained in His clothing for days–perhaps even until He stood before Pilate. Mary was protecting and encouraging His heart bringing Him life even as He was challenging death. Jesus, the son of Joseph and Mary, who was a daughter of Eve, was about to fight the decisive battle in the war between life and death. Everything since has been mopping up battles. The fury against the daughters of Eve has been vented with added ferocity ever since, because Satan knows that he was defeated at the cross. He will do all he can to take down as many of God's precious people as possible before Jesus returns. Jesus changed history and time both physically and spiritually. We, the sons and daughters of Adam and Eve are the prize, the targets. We didn't enlist for this war but we can choose which side we will fight for. It is about life or death!

In John 10:10 Jesus said "The thief comes only to steal, kill and destroy; I have come that they might have life and have it to the full". His whole purpose was to bring life as He stated so clearly when He stood up in the synagogue in Nazareth, took the scroll of Isaiah and read the scripture "The Spirit of the Lord is upon Me, because He has anointed Me to preach the gospel to the poor. He has sent Me to proclaim release to the captives, and recovery of sight to the blind, to set free those who are downtrodden, to proclaim the favourable year of the Lord". (Luke 4: 18-19) Jesus set out to bring the love of God to everyone He met. Person after person felt the power of that love and was changed, healed, and set free from every fear, disease or handicap. No one ever before loved the way He loved. The revolution that He brought was that we could love that way too. In loving one another, God and ourselves, we would verify the truth of scripture. As I have read and reread Jesus' high priestly prayer in John 17, I am awestruck with the promises, the glory and all the joy that is open to us. I remember when our daughter Jenny first read John 17:21: "Father I want those You have given Me to be with Me where I am, and to see My glory, the glory You have given Me because You loved Me before the creation of the world". Jenny said "Mum, Jesus wants to have a sleepover–an eternal sleepover!" The wonderful simplicity of a little 10 year old girl!

Here in our country of Canada, we take it for granted that we can own a Bible, or even many Bibles. There are places in the world where having even one page of scripture in your possession could cost you your life. We all owe an enormous debt of gratitude to the Jewish people who have suffered for centuries at Satan's hand because they have faithfully preserved God's holy word. We have become so familiar with the words that we are in danger of falling into unbelief. For believers in China, there have been times when obtaining a Bible was simply impossible, so they dug up the graves of people who had died and whose families had buried their treasured Bibles with them. A man known as Brother Yun fasted for 100 days in order to get his own Bible. He and other believers memorized whole books of scripture because it was too dangerous to have one in one's house. The Chinese believers didn't just read the words–they had to live them. They trusted God to warn them of danger, to heal them when they were hurt or ill because authorized medical care was not available for fugitives. When they were imprisoned they took the love of God into those dark places and brought hope and life to other prisoners and guards alike. They came to feel that the prisons where they were incarcerated were where the Lord trained them to love their enemies and so fulfil the command to love your enemy and do good to him who hates you. (See also Proverbs 25:21, and 24:17) The message of love did not begin in the New Testament but is present in the whole Bible from Genesis to Revelation.

We know from stories we have read about believers in WW II German prisons, that the Lord performed many miracles of provision and protection. Faith motivated by love brought hope, healing and health into those dark places as well. It seems we have to get into life and death situations where we humans cannot possibly rescue ourselves before we will turn to our God and pray with true faith for the help only He can send.

I would like to come back to something I shared earlier. When I said to the Lord that I didn't see any war or danger in Victoria, what He showed me was a war beneath a war; a war of apathy, confusion and ignorance, and a famine of the word of God as the prophet spoke in Amos 8:11. "Behold the days are coming," declares the Lord God, "when I will send a famine on the land, not a famine for bread or a thirst for water, but rather for hearing the words of the Lord." It is an ominous passage. When we look at the statistics on divorce, disease, delinquency and the like I am inclined to ask "Are we there yet?" But something exciting is starting to bubble beneath under the surface that is going to cause many ripples in our thinking and that we need to listen to very carefully.

There is a movement of prayer that is largely under the radar, in schools, hospitals, governments and business that is growing rapidly. It seems small and rather inconsequential at first but the effects are measurable. It is easy to dismiss prayer as we sometimes say things like "all I can do is pray" as though prayer was a last resort, futile sort of thing. There is a mystery here that is beginning to unfold.

We are hearing snippets of how the great god 'science' is being changed by something called 'quantum physics'. Just the word 'physics' is enough to make some of us roll our eyes and glaze over! In many ways this fairly new branch of study is simply proving the Bible to be true. Let me illustrate.

In a experiment whose details I cannot understand, physicists were able to separate electrons that normally work with one another in pairs spinning in ways that complement each other and produce power. The scientists were able to separately manipulate the direction of spin in each electron in a pair. Though they were separated by many miles the other electron of the pair instantly changed the direction of its spin to complement its partner. The fact that they can even measure that change is mind boggling enough but when we realize that there was absolutely no contact between the electrons and no time lag of even milliseconds we have to question what is happening and how.

The quantum experimenters discovered, to their amazement, that there were times when they were expecting a particular outcome in an experiment and it happened exactly as predicted. When they then ran the experiment again expecting the opposite result, they were able by their own thoughts to change the outcome. More and more the expectations of quantum scientists are being challenged to the point that they are now suggesting that there may be no such thing as objective science. When you can change an outcome by what you think and expect, you do have to re-examine the basis of your whole world view.

Now hang on a minute.....Proverbs 23:7 says in the NAS "as a man thinks in his heart so is he." Jesus said in Matthew 21:22 "If you believe you will receive whatever you ask for in prayer." The apostle Paul wrote in Philippians 4:8-9 "Finally brethren, whatever is true, whatever is honourable, whatever is right, whatever is pure, whatever is lovely, whatever is of good repute, if there is any excellence and if anything worthy of praise, let your mind dwell on these things. The things you have learned and received and heard and seen in me, practise these things and the God of peace will be with you." There are many other scriptures along the same theme. Perhaps science is catching up with the Bible!

Many of us have heard about experiments that advocate talking to your plants to encourage them to grow well. Playing good music in barns causes cows to produce more milk. Heavy metal music causes them to stop producing milk altogether. I am beginning to understand that when it says in 2 Corinthians 10:5 "to take captive every thought to make it obedient to Christ" there is a great deal more going on here than meets the eye. It is a true mystery. All the admonitions to be careful about thoughts and words are making more sense the more I learn about all this.

We've all been told, and we agree in our heads, that there is great power in prayer and in our words, thoughts and beliefs. I suspect we really haven't a clue about how much power is available to us nor how we are to use it. Some time ago we watched a DVD called "The Fabric of Time", all about the Shroud of Turin. The Shroud is a 14 foot long piece of fabric with the faint outline of a man who has been scourged and crucified. It has been kept in a cathedral in Turin, Italy for many centuries and venerated as a holy relic. It has been studied, tested and photographed by many, many experts. There have also been many, many arguments about its authenticity. The DVD that was produced from some of the latest investigations states quite categorically that the most modern sophisticated technology has no way of reproducing the image and cannot begin to explain how it was done in the first place so many centuries ago. Furthermore the image is a 3D hologram with the man's back showing no sign of distortion which you would expect of a simple photograph of somebody lying on a stone slab. The inference is that the image was formed at the moment of resurrection power entering the body and lifting it off the stone slab. One of the leading researchers declared this to be a new and previously unknown dimension that changes science and equates to the beginning of the universe and the big bang theory. Our understanding of time, science and everything we thought about death and life are being challenged and changed.

On many fronts our suppositions are being greatly challenged. When Jesus said He had authority to lay down His life and to take it up again in John 10:18, was He giving our generation a clue to what we are beginning to see happen in our day? If our thoughts can have the power to move electrons, what does that suggest about how we could influence the outcomes of disease, weather or even wars? Jesus said: "I only do what My Father tells Me to do." If we could hear the Father as clearly as He did, could we accomplish what Jesus promised to His disciples in John 14:12? "I tell you the truth, anyone who has faith in Me will do what I have been doing and even greater things than these, because I am going to the Father." Do we believe that? We certainly agree in our heads, we hope we can, but thoughts and hopes have to lead into actions.

I want to refer back to Lazarus for a moment. Jesus called him out of the tomb and then told the people standing there to unwrap him. Our Western minds say "of course"! However that culture had very strict laws about touching dead things and they all knew that Lazarus had been dead for four days! Death had been conquered for the time being but it had to be replaced by life and only a change of attitudes, thoughts, expectations, and even religious laws could restore Lazarus to his community.

Perhaps a more recent example of the Lord setting a man free from an impossible situation is what happened in China to Brother Yun. He was once again in prison, but had been severely tortured, beaten, with both his legs broken to prevent him from trying to escape. Other prisoners had to carry him to the toilet and help him to get in and out of bed. One day he clearly heard the Lord tell him to get up and walk; that it was time to leave that prison. He reminded the Lord that his legs were badly broken but the Lord insisted that he get up and leave. So he stood up. To his own utter astonishment the door of his cell opened and he walked out, his broken legs instantly healed. Some of the other prisoners saw him walking but he signalled for them to be very quiet! One door after another in the prison opened as he went through, down three flights of stairs and out on to the street where a taxi was waiting for him. He was taken to a safe house and from there escaped out of China and went first to Germany and then to the United States. This reminds me so much of the account in Acts of an angel appearing to Peter in prison while all the believers were praying for his release. Peter's shackles fell off, the doors opened, and he walked out into the streets. It seems the Lord really meant it when He said He came to set the captives free!

More and more we also are being called to put our faith and belief into practise. In this life and death war our greatest weapon is love— love of God, love of ourselves and love for others. It is not enough just to think. First we must listen and hear the voice of God. He is always speaking but our problem is that we are not always listening. That listening process takes a great deal longer to become a reality in our lives than it does to write it or say it. We must know God's voice and His character which we learn by knowing our Bibles and through prayer and constant practise of listening. Then when our Commander-in-Chief calls us we need to be willing to do His will. We pray: "Thy will be done on earth as it is in heaven." Now we need to be obedient to the voice of our God.

Chapter 11

WHAT IS SPIRITUAL WARFARE?

The summer of 2012 was about the worst summer that I can remember. It certainly wasn't planned that way! The original plan was that our kids would come from Fort McMurray to celebrate Peter's birthday on July 22 and my birthday on July 23 and we would all enjoy some wonderful "family time". It turned out to be one of those 'Murphy' times–just about everything that could go wrong did! One of the few bright spots was the gift they arranged for my birthday–a most unusual gift that probably most people would not appreciate. It was a dual-flush toilet. Perhaps it was even prophetic! We have lived with a low-flow well for many years so such a gift was most thoughtful.

A week or so later on July 31st we returned home about 8 pm after enjoying a barbeque with the other grandparents here in Victoria, to find our German Shepherd, Yael, in great distress. We rushed her to the emergency hospital where she died about seven hours later. She was only 2 years and 8 months old. We were absolutely devastated! She was such a fun companion with a sense of humour and an uncanny knack for knowing exactly what was expected. She was the most intelligent dog we have ever had and we just could not understand what had happened. She was also a dog we had put a great deal of extra time into. She had developed a very serious liver condition when she was about six months old and we spent many hours nursing her, feeding her and praying over her. Every meal we managed to get into her was a triumph. Every pill we got her to swallow and stay down was a victory. We were attached to her in extraordinary ways.

There were five extra people in the house and there was so much coming and going and we just didn't have the time or space to properly grieve for our very special friend. We just had to keep going. There were meals to make, kids to drive to day-camps, and Peter and Shauna back and forth to the airport so they could continue to go to work. Peter decided to replace the front stairs of our house–which desperately needed to be done–but it added greatly to the busyness, mess and confusion.

That summer was very hot and there was no rain for a long, long time. Our well pump was acting up and needed to be fixed even though we had replaced the pump less than a year before. The technician was away on holiday and it took a few days for the man who was filling in to be able to come to fix it. The well was already being strained with all the extra people, dishes, baths, toilet flushing and then..... we ran out of water. So Peter installed two more dual-flush toilets to help the situation, for which we are very grateful. That also meant more confusion and mess as some bathrooms were unusable for a few days and three used toilets were stacked up outside the front door alongside the driveway. Not at all a pretty sight to come home to nor very welcoming either!

Into the middle of this ballygan (the word means a mess) the childcare arrangement in Fort McMurray fell apart. So in order to stay working, Peter and Shauna asked if the kids could stay here in Victoria with us, and start school here until they could work things out with some childcare. Foolishly we said yes. There was a lot of extra laundry, which I had to take to the Laundromat, and extra grocery shopping. It didn't take long before I was looking and feeling like an angry, crabby, grumpy, nasty, old lady! Our doctor, pastors, as well as many friends said very plainly and forcefully "YOU CAN'T DO THIS ANYMORE!"

Then one Friday our grandson, Eli, came home from school with a very bad headache and a high fever. He was no better on Saturday and by the evening he was complaining of a pain in his neck. I took him to emergency. As I was sitting there I was wondering "how long would it take for this child's parents to get here from Fort McMurray? If he has something seriously wrong–and I was thinking meningitis which can cause death in just a few hours–could they get here in less than a day?"

A decision was made to take the children back to Fort McMurray after much anger, miscommunication, offence, both taken and given and misunderstanding on both sides. I was absolutely exhausted and slept for 12 hours without waking once!

I had registered months earlier to go to a Ladies Retreat the first weekend in November and I was so tired I really thought of cancelling. But my friend Mary also wanted to go and I was her transportation so we went. I really was not thinking of doing much other than sleeping but God had other ideas.

I have noticed over the years, that the Lord often allows me to go through a situation first and <u>then</u> teaches me about how He would prefer that I handle it. Our speaker was Isabel Allum, a prophetic lady from Ontario, originally from Costa Rica. During one of her talks she told about something that had happened to her when she was on a teaching trip to Germany.

She had already done one week of teaching in a former West German town and was to go next to a town in what had been East Germany. She had to stay overnight in the first town and was to be billeted with a couple from the church. That night the couple had the worst fight–in three languages–English, German and Finnish. The man got horribly drunk on wine and vodka and was still drunk the next morning. In the morning, when they were to leave the woman drove because the man was still drunk and not a happy kind of drunk either! They set out for East Germany but along the way they had to stop for gas and Mr Drunk fell and hurt himself. His wife decided to take him to the nearest hospital. That meant hours of delay. As the day stretched on, Isabel realized that she was not going to get to the next venue in time to have dinner with the new pastors and committee at the next church. In fact she wasn't going to get much to eat the whole day. But through the whole ordeal she kept thinking, "All this mess is not my problem. My Father knows what is happening to me and He is in charge. I don't need to take offence." She found a box of nectarines in the car, and the drunk's wine bottle–which she considered drinking herself–but otherwise had nothing to eat all day. She had no idea where she was so it was not like she could just take a bus, or walk or rent a car for herself. Her job was to trust God and know that the Father was going to get her safely to where He needed her to be. She missed the dinner with the new pastors and went to bed eventually, relieved but quite exhausted. It had been a long day but at no time did she take offence at all the frustrating circumstances.

The next day she met the pastors and committee who had arranged the conference. It was a very small church group–11 people in all–who had organized the event. Seventy people had registered and they had managed to rent the Town Hall for the occasion. As Isabel was going up the beautiful staircase to enter the building, she saw that there were angels all along the stairs and as she passed they all bowed. The hassle of the day before started to make a bit more sense as she felt the Lord's presence.

That week was wonderful. The people were very receptive and everything went well. The gospel was preached, the people responded, the church grew and Isabel left that town at the end of the week, feeling tired but content that she had done what the Father had sent her to do. She went back to "West" Germany to get a plane back to Canada but this time stayed in a hotel for the night.

She was sitting on the bed in the hotel room when the Lord walked right through the door and sat down beside her. He looked pleased and said to her "We did it!" "What did 'we' do Lord?" She found out later that the Town Hall where they had been was where Hitler had planned the extermination of the Jews and the gas they had used had been developed in that town. The angels had been waiting there all that time and looking forward to being able to release the people from that demonic captivity that prevented God's salvation from flourishing in that place. Suddenly Isabel realized how very imperative it had been that she not take offence during that awful frustrating day with the arguing woman, her drunken husband and nothing to eat.

Now, I know as well as you do that Jesus does not teach us things in order to condemn us but I felt very convicted by that story. During a bit of a quiet time I asked the Lord, with some exasperation, "Why didn't You teach all that to me before the children came for their visit?" He replied, "This is the pattern I have used with you for many years; you don't easily forget after you have experienced this kind of lesson." I had certainly felt great offence at the presumption and entitlement spirit of my son, daughter-in-law, and my grandchildren. I had been, not just annoyed but really angry, far too often. I asked the Lord to forgive my selfish, bad temper and all the offence I had both taken and given. I was very thankful that the Lord had not called me to bring His gospel to rescue a town because I had blown it terribly. I also realized that at times friends had taken offence on our behalf because of what we had tried to do when thinking we were helping Peter and Shauna.

It seems such a small thing, this matter of offence, but it is not. On later reflection I realized something that should have been very obvious much earlier. Even though we had talked frequently on the telephone we did not have an adult to adult relationship with our kids. We did not have enough common experiences as adults together, such as going to dinner, or the movies, or a picnic or a holiday to be able to put such a strain on our relationship. We were still "mum and dad" in their thinking–the people who provide what is needed. To us they were still our kids–the ones we were to look after. I also realized much later, that the time when we should have been establishing those experiences that would promote adult to adult relationship was at the time of Paul's accident. The kids were just moving from teen years to leaving home and becoming more independent. There was a period of five years, five very critical years, when Paul was almost silent. Virtually the only emotion he could express during that time was anger–definitely not conducive to developing happy relationships. Much of the time he sat with his eyes closed lacking the energy to engage or participate. Brain injuries are extremely difficult to understand or have much empathy over. You can't put a plaster cast on your head for a damaged cerebellum.

Within a few weeks of their departure we had enough sense to truly forgive our kids and grandkids but that was not the end of the problem. Nor was it just that we had given and taken offence. It took quite some time but eventually I realized–slow learner that I am–that I had not applied the four-step 'ezer knegdo' remedy to the dilemma. The first step was to identify the enemy. And no, it was not Peter and Shauna. As always, it was Satan. Step two was identifying his tactics. We had been kept overwhelmed with busyness, confusion, bad communication and emotional turmoil. Both Paul and I are in our 70's and no longer used to living with a lot of noise and confusion. There was Yael's sudden death, five extra people in the house, running out of water, too much extra work with meals, laundry and driving. I felt like a terrible failure. I had been teaching about God's four step program for dealing with crises for ten years but I didn't recognize it when it hit us so hard. Exhaustion and offence had won another victory for Satan!

You know how sometimes when you learn something new all of a sudden you are seeing it everywhere you turn? This is how it seems to be for me as I reflect on the whole issue of offence. In Luke 9:51-56 it says: "As the time approached for Him to be taken up to heaven, Jesus resolutely set out for Jerusalem, and He sent messengers on ahead. They went into a Samaritan village to get things ready for Him, but the people did not welcome Him, because He was heading for Jerusalem. When the disciples James and John saw this, they asked, "Lord do you want us to call down fire from heaven to destroy them?" But Jesus rebuked them. And He said, You do not know what kind of spirit you are of, for the Son of Man did not come to destroy men's lives, but to save them.' And they went to another village."

When we take offence we are looking for retribution. We want to justify ourselves and our bad attitudes whether we are offended ourselves or on behalf of another. Please note that I am not talking about huge personal hurts like murder, rape, robbery or the like. Mostly offence comes from much more minor grievances.

Perhaps another biblical example will help. In Luke 7 John the Immerser was in prison and feeling a little unsure of his situation. He sent some of his disciples to Jesus and asked, "Are you the one who was to come, or should we expect someone else?" Jesus said to the men to go back to His cousin and tell him "The blind receive sight, the lame walk, those who have leprosy are cured, the deaf hear, the dead are raised, and the good news is preached to the poor. *Blessed is the man who is not offended because of me"*. *(My emphasis added)* Matt 11:5. There are at least two really important things to note in this passage. The first is that when Jesus was telling John all the things He was doing, He was saying that these were the messianic miracles that the rabbis were supposed to be watching for that would prove who the true messiah was by what he was doing. Jesus was reassuring John that John's life's work had indeed been accomplished as Zechariah, John's father, had prophesied when he was born. Go back to Luke 2:67-79 and read, with wonder, the amazing prophecy that was pronounced over a newborn son. Secondly Jesus was saying that refusing to take offence carries a blessing with it. In Isabel's experience that was certainly true. By not being offended by the antics of a very dysfunctional couple, Isabel was free to work with Jesus and the Holy Spirit to break off the effects of the sin that had held people captive in that city for many decades. She was enabled to 'preach the good news to the poor' and bring enormous blessing to many.

In Song of Songs there is an interesting little verse that has often puzzled me. In chapter 2:15 it says "Catch for us the foxes, the little foxes that ruin our vineyards that are in blossom." It doesn't seem at first glance to be related to anything else in the passage but in fact it is talking about the distractions that keep us from staying on track with our Lord, our eternal Lover. That is what offences do. They keep us off track and concentrating on a 'rock or stone of stumbling'. We take offence so often we don't even notice anymore. When something goes wrong, from our point of view of course, we immediately look for who is responsible, who can we blame. We automatically determine to avoid that person in the future and it breaks fellowship. We are so in the habit of laying blame and passing judgement that we no longer realize what that does to our relationships.

The vineyard that is in blossom does not yet have fruit growing or ripening so getting distracted right at the beginning prevents the fullness of harvest that the Gardener is looking for. We are all longing to live fruitful lives but we are not helping the process by continuing to carry offences that chop off God's plans before they have even started to grow. We need to learn to recognise and catch those little foxes.

A prime example of the effects of taking offence is found in Mark 6:5. Jesus grew up in the town of Nazareth and was known by all the townsfolk as the carpenter, the son of Mary and Joseph. Everybody knew His brothers and sisters as well. When Jesus stood up in the synagogue and took to Himself the Isaiah 61:1-3 prophecy of the position of Messiah, the good townsfolk demanded "who does this guy think he is. We know his mum and dad and all the rest of his family." Mark writes, "And they took offence at him." In verse 5 it says "He could not do any miracles there, except lay his hands on a few sick people and heal them. And he was amazed at their lack of faith". Today we think that laying hands on a few people IS doing a miracle. I have to wonder how much more we could be doing if we were not so full of offences.

I want to go back to what Jesus said to James and John, those beloved Sons of Thunder, in Luke 9, where He says that He did not come to destroy men's lives but to save them. It is a certainty that offence puts barriers up between people and destroys relationships but it also breaks down societal values as well. In the story of the woman taken in the act of adultery in John 8:1-11, there is the beginning of a mob scene with men threatening Jesus and wanting to stone the woman to death. They had taken serious offence to what the woman had done, flouting, as they believed, the laws of Moses. I, like so many thousands of other people, have wondered often what Jesus wrote with His finger in the dust. Isn't it interesting that Jesus/God's finger wrote in the dust, the very substance He had used to create people in the first place? That same finger had inscribed the original commandments on the stone tablets that those scribes and Pharisees were now using to try to entrap Jesus and condemn Him as well. The Teachers of the law and Pharisees were enraged because the woman had broken the law but they were more than willing to also break the law by committing murder. They also neglected to bring the other party to the adultery as the same law required. They saw keeping laws as the way to keep community order. But Jesus displayed the higher law of divine love that not only prevented those men from breaking the Mosaic laws but also restored the woman to a place where she could change her behaviour to become a valued member of a more wholesome community. He overcame their offences with love just as He had told James and John that He had come to do.

There is also a further more subtle possibility. There is a verse in Jeremiah 17:13, that states: "O Lord, the hope of Israel, all who forsake You will be put to shame. Those who turn away from You will be written in the dust because they have forsaken the Lord, the spring of living water." The older men, who were the first to drop their stones and leave, knew perfectly well that they should have had the adulterous man there facing accusations also. They may have recognized that they were trying to apply God's law very unrighteously and were in danger of having their own names written in the dust that could be blown away with just a puff of wind.

Overcoming the habit of taking offence is not just a matter of 'playing nice'. I know that some of you reading these words are dealing with very difficult situations in your homes and workplaces. Especially if the problems involve family members this is anything but simple and easy. We have not heard from our Fort McMurray family since they left in October 2012. They have taken very great offence at us. Nonetheless God deals with me first. How can I ask Him to soften their hearts when my own is still hurt and angry? How can I expect them to change if my attitude is still holding on to offences? Where there is offence the Lord cannot work many miracles and right now I can't see anything less than a miracle that will restore relationship with our children.

I hope you will recall that when Isabel was having her terrible day she kept reminding herself that the Father knew exactly what was happening and He was responsible for getting her through to a place of victory. She lives with such a certainty of her relationship with the Father that the little distractions of life no longer cause her to take offence at other peoples issues.

I can't remember now whether I read it or heard it but a question came into my mind one day, while I was contemplating this whole issue of offences, and it really bewildered me. 'How do angels and demons fight and where does that happen?' In Revelation chapter 12 there is a description of a great war that seems to be continuing between angels and demons. But there are few details about the connection between what happens in the heavenlies and what happens here on earth.

I have absolutely no doubt that we are living in a spiritual battleground and scripture tells us that much of that battle happens in our minds. That is quite clear and is the reason we have been given the helmet of salvation to protect our thinking. But that helmet doesn't stop the warfare from occurring or continuing. So what is the process and how does it all happen. Because it is pretty apparent that at least part of the reason why evangelism is so hard in many places is because there is a lot of interference in people's thinking.

When I pray, the Lord often speaks to me in pictures. It is rather like watching a TV screen without the sound. Sometimes things are obvious but at other times some commentary would be very helpful. So as I prayed about this issue of where warfare occurs, the Lord showed me something that is difficult to describe. I saw at one level of the screen the kind of stuff that is going on around us all the time–accidents, wars, arguments, bank robberies, illness, emergencies in hospitals–just everyday stuff that cause stress and heartache. Then above that, sort of on a second screen, I saw angels and demons fighting but at first I couldn't see their weapons. Immediately above that I saw a very calm, serene scene of the third heaven where there was order and deliberate planning going on.

A day or so later, we were reading a chapter in Asher Intrater's book "Who Ate Lunch With Abraham?" and a couple of paragraphs jumped off the page at me.

> "This victory reminds us of the 'victory' of Yehoshaphat over the Ammonites and the Moabites (2Chron. 20). He received a prophecy saying that he did not need to fight the battle. The Lord Himself would do the fighting (v15). All they had to do was stand there and believe (v17). The people went out with musical instruments and began to praise the Lord in front of their enemies (v21). As soon as they began to praise the Lord in song, God brought a supernatural victory over their enemies (v22).
>
> The people did not do the essential part of the fighting. The one who fought the battles was the Commander of the Army of Yehovah, along with all His warrior angels. Spiritual warfare is not military warfare alone. Nor is it spirituality disconnected from a military situation. Spiritual warfare is the connection between the heavenly armies and the earthly ones. Our prayers, prophecies and praise affect angels, who in turn affect the military, economic and political situation around us." (page 68)

Using this illustration from Asher Intrater, what I was able to understand about my peculiar picture of the three 'heavens' is this. Just using the small example of taking offence results in breaking relationship with another member of the human race–possibly even a close family member–and now the kingdom of heaven cannot form on earth as it is supposed to. That break is caused by an enemy angel (a demon if you like) lobbing an 'offence bomb' at one of us which we catch and use to break fellowship. That damages the purposes of the heavenly army. If we decline to catch the 'offence bomb' the enemy angels lose that round. I realize that this is a very simplistic explanation but just bear with me as we look at some more scripture.[1]

If we go all the way back to the Garden of Eden we find a terrific war going on between the heavenly angels and Satan and his crew. It was right at the beginning when everything was perfect that Eve took offence at God, Adam took offence at Eve and God, Eve then took offence at Adam and the enemy of their souls had a field day! The first couple could not remain in the perfect place that God had designed for them and had to be protected from the tree of life so that they would not eat it's fruit and live eternally in their sin. They were removed from the Garden and cherubim with a flaming sword was placed at the gate to prevent their re-entry. Warfare came to earth!

---

[1] Who Ate Lunch With Abraham? A study of the appearances of God in the form of a Man in the Hebrew Scriptures by Asher Intrater, published by Intermedia Publishing Group 2011, Peoria, Arizona, U.S.A.

We know from scripture what was happening here on earth for many hundreds of years but it isn't until we get to Isaiah 14 and Daniel 8 that we learn about the war in heaven that began before mankind was created. The mighty angel Lucifer, who wanted to exalt himself above the throne of God, caused a revolt among the angels and a third of the heavenly host was thrown down to the second heaven where they were confined, along with Lucifer, who was renamed Satan, and the terrible war against mankind really exploded. It did not take long before murder was added to the sins of the first family and the warfare escalated.

Adam and Eve were told by God in Genesis 1:28, to "be fruitful and increase in number; fill the earth and subdue it". My goodness, we have done a great job of the increasing part of that command. It is very interesting that right at the beginning when they were to go out to inhabit the earth and establish God's kingdom the first couple came under satanic attack. Fellowship between God and man was broken.

Many years go by and again people were sent into a territory to establish a place for God's kingdom and they came under spiritual warfare again when they attempted to go into the Promised Land. The people took offence against Moses for taking them into the wilderness to die. "Were there not enough graves in Egypt?" was their complaint. They complained about the water and the food and even Moses wife! There seemed to be no end to the offences that were being thrown their way by demonic interference. Moses also was told to speak to the rock but instead took offence at the rebellious people and struck the rock. The leadership was then removed from him and given to Joshua. Even so, God did not change His overall plan. All the tribes of Israel were told to go into the land, to teach their children all that the Lord had commanded and to prosper as they took possession of the land God had promised to their forefathers.

There is absolutely no doubt that they were as unaware of the spiritual battles going on around and above them as we are in our day. God gave the people very specific instructions of how they were to resolve the differences between themselves, how they were to worship Him, what they were to eat, who they should and should not marry and many, many other rules to keep their community safe and harmonious. Reading the book of Leviticus is a challenge unless you understand what God is trying to teach the Israelites. It is interesting to note that God does not spell out in any of the early books where the real source of all their strife was coming from.

When we come to the New Testament we hear, in the Sermon on the Mount, Jesus re-interpreting but not changing, the Ten Commandments. For many of us the words hardly sound like the same thing at all. The negatives are put in positive terms–love your neighbour, feed the hungry, be merciful, seek righteousness, be humble, worship God alone.

At the very end of the book of Matthew Jesus said "Therefore go and make disciples of all nations, baptizing them in the name of the Father and of the Son and of the Holy Spirit and teaching them to obey everything I have commanded you." In New Testament terms this is a reiteration of the command to Adam and Eve "to be fruitful and multiply". We are to make disciples, not converts, to multiply ourselves–the fruitful part involves teaching others everything Jesus commanded.

We are pretty good at making converts but disciples are rather different. As I was listening to Joel Rosenberg one day he said that we should all be being discipled AND then discipling someone younger in the faith than we are. That is true multiplication. That involves a great deal more than going to church on Sundays and listening to a sermon. At its very core it requires building relationship with another human being. Almost as soon as we determine to have a relationship with someone there will be spiritual interference!

Up to now the whole issue of discipleship training has been a minefield of misunderstandings. It does not mean one person controlling another. It does not mean creating dependencies so that every decision must be channelled through another. It is not about creating hierarchies. It is really a lot more like "please allow me to share with you what I have learned so far on my journey?" I have heard it described as 'one beggar telling another beggar where to find food.' Again that is a pretty simplistic explanation but it is a start.

Most of us are fairly comfortable with the thought of being a disciple. That involves serving, learning, making friends with Jesus and hopefully, with other disciples. But how do we feel about **making** disciples? That involves maturity, responsibility, time invested and spent with others and daily seeking wisdom from the Lord on behalf of a disciple. That is not nearly so comfortable. I am terribly aware that I have no qualifications of my own that enable me to bring God's words to even one of those whom I love dearly. Most of us are happy to seek someone who will mentor or disciple us but turning the thing around and doing it for a beginner is really daunting. What if I fail that new believer? What if I tell them something that isn't true? You can fill in all your own 'what if's' but be aware that the 'what if' game is one of Satan's favourite daggers aimed right at your heart! The important thing to realize is that the process requires us/me to allow the Holy Spirit to work through me to bless the new disciple. I don't have to do it on my own. As I am submitted to Jesus, He then is able to fight His battle through me to defeat whatever the enemy is trying to throw in the path of the new believer. Because Jesus loves unconditionally, we too must learn to love unconditionally. It is impossible to love unconditionally if we/I am holding on to offences to use just a 'small' example.

All of that is spiritual warfare because we are getting very close to the time when we will take back the whole earth that belongs to our God. There has never been a time before now that we have been more aware of spiritual warfare all around us. The Holy Spirit was sent to teach us all things including how to co-operate with the armies of heaven to defeat Satan's forces and all his plans, his little foxes that ruin the vineyards. Every time God sent His people into a new land there was warfare, both spiritual and actual. As Asher Intrater said, "Our prayers, prophecies and praise affect angels, who in turn, affect the military, economic and political situation all around us."[2] Two Corinthians 10:4-6 says that we do not fight with worldly weapons but effective spiritual weapons that can demolish pretensions and take captive thoughts and arguments. Bullets don't have much effect on demons but the word of God certainly does. We need to be able to understand more clearly the integration between the work of the armies of God and our obedience to the call of Jesus on our lives.

The Lord's plan is for us to partner with Him in establishing His kingdom here on earth as it is in heaven. It is not just a business type of partnership He is looking for. It is so much more. He wants friends, special friends; the kind of friend that is a marriage partner of the very best sort.

---

[2] Ibid

Developing a friendship with Jesus is the best way to overcome all the insidious things that cause the breakdown of fellowship and therefore prevent the building of the Kingdom. Abraham, Moses, David and many others were counted as God's friends and were able to change the course of history because of that friendship. Keeping His commandments is not duty–it's friendship.

Too often we try to fix situations, but friendship with Jesus–which is what He said He wanted with us–means being able to say "Jesus, here is the mess I'm in. What do You want to do about it?" Our pastor Bruce, has been teaching about the goodness of God in our lives. Doubt brings God's goodness into question and makes it very difficult for us to stand on the rock of His love. We reflect what we believe about what God believes about us/me. Is He disappointed in the mess I made of my relationship with my kids? No, He knows what is in me, what needs to be changed and grown and how best to do that changing and growing. The Lord is not done with me yet and to the degree that I co-operate with Him He will be able to change and redeem my circumstances. That does not mean, necessarily, that my relationship with my children will be restored. It certainly does guarantee that my relationship with Jesus and the Father will strengthen, deepen and become very life giving. It will also bring joy and glory to my Saviour and Redeemer, Jesus.

In order to overcome this affliction of offence we must start by knowing that God is good and that He loves me and you. We need to be certain that all His plans for each of us are good. We also need to be certain that He is very capable of making all His plans come to pass at the right time and in the right way. Precious Jesus, come now and teach us more about trusting You, being Your friend, and having You be our/my friend.

Chapter 12
WEAPONS OF MASS CONSTRUCTION

One of my favourite pastimes is quilting. It is quiet, creative, and I can think of things as I sew. One afternoon the Lord interrupted my concentration and said, "Ask Me for weapons of mass CONstruction." The next question, of course, was "What weapons do You want to highlight Lord?" Does the Lord ever answer your question with another question? He answered, "How many would you like to start with?" So I just picked what seemed like a good number..."Five please." I've since thought of many more but here are the five He gave me to start. Waiting. Fellowship/relationship. Covenant. Purity. Hope. At first some of these didn't really seem to be weapons but He reminded me of 2 Cor 10:4, "The weapons we fight with are not the weapons of the world. On the contrary they have divine power to demolish strongholds."

We tend to think of waiting as a very passive state but it really isn't. In the movie 'Brave Heart', William Wallace was leading a group of Scottish peasants in a revolt against the English who controlled the land and all it produced. The Scots had no weapons but the English had swords and were on horses. There is a powerful scene where the

English had backed the Scots into a wooded area and knew that with their superior weapons, they could defeat those unarmed rebels. The Scots were lying on the ground with their faces painted with blue woad, armed with the only thing they could fight with–poles. Just wooden poles sharpened to a point at one end. As the English charged at them Wallace said, "Wait. Wait until they are right upon us." At the last possible moment they lifted up their sharpened poles and the horses and riders drove themselves at full speed onto the deadly Scottish weapons.

There are actually about 25 different words in scripture that are used to mean wait. Some have the suggestion of laying in ambush, as William Wallace did, while some mean to be silent and still. Some mean to have hope and expectancy. Some suggest a gathering together and to survey, observe or spy out the land. There are quite a number of places in scripture where we are told to wait. Ps 27:14 "Wait for the Lord, be strong and take heart and wait for the Lord." Ps 130:5-6 "I will wait for the Lord, my soul waits, and in His word I put my hope. My soul waits for the Lord more than watchmen wait for the morning, more than watchmen wait for the morning." Isa 30:18 "Yet the Lord longs to be gracious to you; He rises to show you compassion. For the Lord is a God of justice. Blessed are all who wait for Him!" There is a blessing for those who wait for the leading of the Lord!

To Satan, waiting for something makes no sense at all. He has no patience so he will do everything he can to get us to move too quickly. He will always offer a shortcut, a quick solution to whatever our dilemma is. Just one example is the worldwide financial mess that most countries are in, largely based on a brilliant (but unrighteous) advertising campaign to "Buy now. Pay later." Satan can then get us to spend time worrying about all our debts instead of trusting God for all we need. I realize that for some people credit cards have become almost essential but for too many people it is no longer the necessities that go on the credit card but rather 'things' that bring instant self gratification. When we become prosperous there is a danger of forgetting that it is the Lord who supplies all our needs not necessarily our wants.

I learned about waiting being a weapon one day when I was praying for my brother, David. At the time I didn't even know where he was living. I told the Lord that I really wanted my brother to be in heaven with me when I get there; that somehow if David wasn't there, then there would be something missing. The Lord invited me to come and stand at the gate with the Father and pray as the father of the prodigal son had prayed. He didn't promise that my brother would come home. He didn't say that everything would work out well. He just invited me to keep the Father company and pray. It took about five years of praying every day but one day my brother phoned me and that was the beginning of many reconciliations for him. He still has a very long way to go but he now tells me that he and the Lord are on a first name basis though they don't talk very often.

That kind of waiting with the Father is not passive. It is not about doing nothing, just sitting around waiting for something to happen. It requires perseverance and focus. It also requires trusting the Lord in the face of nothing obvious happening.

There is another kind of waiting that is also a major weapon in this fight. If you worked in a restaurant and Jesus came in and ordered a meal, I guarantee that every employee in the place would want to 'wait' on Him. What an honour to pour a glass of water for Him. It would be tempting to pile His plate high with triple the amount of food. If He happened to drop His fork we would all be bumping heads trying to be the first to pick it up and give Him a clean one.

But what happens when we see an injustice, or poverty, or abuse of women or children, or any of the other many, many things that spoil this magnificent world He created? How do we serve Him then? How often do we ask, "Lord what do You need me to do for You today?" then really listen for His answer. A kind word. A phone call. Forgive a deliberate slight. Pray. Just sit quietly and adore Him. That last one is very hard to do in our crazy world but it blesses His heart so much.

The second weapon we will look at is fellowship and relationship with one another. We talked earlier about God saying that it was not good for the man to be alone–especially during the cosmic war that Adam didn't seem to be aware of. There is a big difference between being alone and being lonely. Being alone is about circumstances but being lonely is about attitudes. You can be lonely in a crowd because you choose not to engage with other people.

In Ecck 4:12, it says, "Though one may be over powered, two can defend themselves. A cord of three strands is not quickly broken." In that same chapter we read in verses 9–11 "Two are better than one because they have a good return for their work. If one falls down, his friend can help him up. But pity the man who falls and has no one to help him up! Also, if two lie down together, they will keep warm. But how can one keep warm alone?" We all recognize the benefits of working together and the synergy of added strength when we work together. Also fairly obvious, is the explosion of fresh ideas and the exchange of inspiration in co-operative effort. Our Bible is crammed full of admonitions to stay connected to one another. So why do we need so much prodding when it is to our benefit? We were made for relationship since we are 'image bearers' and within the Trinity (whose image we bear) there is eternal relationship. If there was ever division between the Father, the Son and Holy Spirit everything would cease to be. John 1:3 tells us, "All things came into being by Him; and apart from Him nothing came into being that has come into being." Heb 1:3, "This Son is the radiance of the Sh'khinah, the very expression of God's essence, upholding all that exists by His powerful word; and after He had, through Himself made purification for sins, He sat down at the right hand of the majesty on high." (Complete Jewish Bible) It is the love relationship of the Godhead that causes all things to continue to exist.

Satan has many tricks to keep us from whole-heartedly embracing relationships. He has learned to use division, suspicion, gossip, fear, envy, misunderstandings, offence and a host of other tactics to keep us from forming unbreakable relationships. He knows that if we ever get to the point where men and women not only agree to work together to bring the kingdom of heaven to earth but actually start to do it, then he is finished as the prince of the air on planet earth.

When Jesus was on the cross and asked the Father to forgive all of us because we didn't know what we were doing, Satan must have let out a howl that could be heard from one side of the galaxy to the other. The power of forgiveness can break curses, reverse disease, shatter strongholds and bring resurrection. Jesus proved it then and He still proves it time and time again even to this day.

Forgiveness is one part of the power of fellowship and unity is another very important element that confounds Satan's schemes. When the people of Babel were building their tower, God Himself said, "Here they are, one people with a single language, and now they have started to do this; henceforward nothing they have a mind to do will be beyond their reach." This is not just about everybody's effort and strength being channelled to a useful purpose. There is real power in unity that goes far beyond mere effort. Unity has within it the whole dynamic of trust. The word fellowship itself comes from the old Anglo-Saxon word "fellmonger" which means a dealer in hides. It was the practice in Medieval Europe for the peasants to herd their cattle together for safety and security. But your cattle represented your wealth and in order to keep everybody's livestock together they had to really trust each other with their wealth. How much would we trust our neighbours with our wealth? How many of us even know our neighbours? Unity is sadly lacking in our societies–even in our families. We are such a highly mobile, individualistic culture now that for most of us we have totally lost touch with our roots and heritage.

The third weapon the Lord spoke to me about was covenant. Our Bibles are full of the bewildering elements of covenant. Abraham cut animals into two pieces and laid them on the ground and then fought off birds of prey until a smoking brazier moved between them. David and Jonathan exchanged coats and weapons. There are many other examples. What we don't understand, we will not value. But our God is a covenant keeping God so we need to know and understand what He is laying down for us as principles for effective living.

Here very briefly are the elements of covenant:

1. Exchange of weapons
2. Exchange of coats or clothes
3. Exchange of names
4. Mixing of blood by cutting our wrists or arms
5. We make a scar
6. Exchange of tokens or rings
7. Sharing a meal which includes bread and wine
8. We establish a memorial

When you consider all these elements, the most obvious ceremony we have in today's society that fills these criteria is the marriage ceremony. For God a covenant is unbreakable but we treat covenants as a business deal that is useful if convenient and to our advantage. If a marriage doesn't work out, we'll just get a divorce and start over with somebody else. Yes, it hurts but that's life. Right? No! The hurt is deep and very traumatic as many people can attest. Covenants have a power that can defeat Satan's efforts to divide and conquer. Our marriages are supposed to mirror the expected marriage of Jesus to His pure, spotless Bride. We need to learn about the sacredness of covenants because it is a very powerful, effective weapon that can defeat the enemy's efforts to sabotage the Blessed Alliance that the Lord God intended when He created Adam and Eve.

But I want us to personalize this issue of covenant. So please close your eyes, make yourself quiet and come with me to a lonely hill outside ancient Jerusalem. We are standing in front of Jesus' cross. He is there but at the moment He is not suffering because He wants to talk just with you. Nobody else is around. It is just you and Jesus. Quietly He starts to speak.

"I want you to lay down all your weapons and use Mine instead. All your frustration, anger, shame and guilt are weapons that have been used against you. I want you to use My weapons instead."

"My robe is lying on the ground near your feet. Take it and wear it and leave your own clothes that are full of sin in place of My seamless garment. In My robe you will be covered with My righteousness and purity."

"Listen carefully and I will give you a new name that will reflect the new way that you will live from this day forward. You will experience new birth so you will need a new name."

"Do you see My blood? My blood has great power to cleanse you from all sin both in your thoughts and your deeds. Treasure My blood. It will defeat every trick My enemy tries to use to make you stumble."

"In a few days when I return in a new body there will be scars on my hands, feet and sides. They are scars of triumph and honour just as your own scars are signs of overcoming when you follow My path and suffer for My sake."

"When you join Me in My Father's house there is waiting for you a crown that will be a token of My love for you."

"Remember Me every time you sit down to eat. There is joy in sharing bread and wine."

"Every Shabbat we will participate together to share this memorial feast with the whole community who has chosen to put their trust in Me. Bless you My precious daughter."

Seven hundred years before Jesus was born Jeremiah prophesied in chapters 31 to 34, "Behold the days are coming declares the Lord, when I will make a new covenant with the house of Israel and the house of Judah,....But this is the covenant I will make with the house of Israel after those days," declares the Lord, "I will put My law within them, and on their hearts I will write it; and I will be their God and they shall be My people." Jesus made that new covenant with us, that we celebrate as Holy Communion, and He urged us to remember Him every time we eat and drink at that feast.

What an old fashioned word is 'purity'. In our culture a very old fashioned idea too. It conjures up pictures of ladies dressed in very prim high-necked dresses that fall to their ankles. Preferably dull gray. But that is not what the Bible means by purity.

I wonder how many readers are old enough to remember the advertisements for Ivory Snow laundry soap–99 & 44/100th percent pure! Almost perfect! But for God almost is not enough. Here is the best news of all. Father God knows that by ourselves we can't be perfect–or noble, or pure so He planned from before the foundation of the world that He Himself would come and wash us in His own blood that takes away all sin no matter how bad we might think we are. All we have to do is ask! The enemy would like us to believe that His sacrifice might apply to everybody else but we are too bad. It can't mean me. That is a lie but we need one another to reinforce the truth. Jesus' sacrifice of Himself was so effective that it says in Hebrews 1:3, "After He had provided purification for sins, He sat down at the right hand of the Majesty in heaven."

Psalm 119:9 asks "How can a young man keep his way pure? By living according to Your word." Hab 1:13 says, "Your eyes are too pure to look on evil." Phil 4:8 "Finally brothers, (and sisters) whatever is true, whatever is noble, whatever is right, whatever is pure, whatever is lovely, whatever is admirable–if anything is excellent or praiseworthy–think about such things." Your concordance will direct you to many other places where we are urged to concentrate on 'purity' because what we will fill our minds with and allow to pass before our eye gates will inevitably influence what we speak and do. When we put on the whole armour of God every morning we are urged to put on the helmet of salvation. Your mind is the major battle ground where most of the attacks of the enemy will be directed. If you refuse to indulge in watching, or listening to, or thinking about, or participating in activities that you could not do with Jesus, then the enemy will not be able to lead you into sin.

There is another side to this issue of purity as well. If you aim for a pure life you will influence others to follow your lead. Only you can–and should–set the standard of how you intend to live your life.

This is actually part of the original mandate God gave in the Garden of Eden to "fill the earth and subdue it"–purity of thoughts, words and deeds cannot help but subdue (defeat) God's enemy. For the reward of a life lived in purity read Matt 5:8, "Blessed are the pure in heart for they will see God."

Hope is the fifth weapon the Lord highlighted to me and one that I have struggled with most often. The kind of hope the Lord is talking about is not 'wishful thinking'. It has much more substance than that. It is one of the three things that will remain after prophecies cease, tongues are stilled and knowledge passes away. (See 1 Cor 13:13)

For most of us, especially in this day, we want to understand things before we can believe. But hundreds of years ago St Anselm (I believe) said, "I believe therefore I understand." Hope is a bit like that. Hope requires us to put our trust in Jesus, in order to touch Him, or hear Him. Hope says that Jesus has been this way before and He will lead me to a safe place if I trust Him. It isn't a 'hope against hope' but a sure thing. Jesus has the blueprint and is a Master Builder so we can be certain that since He is the Light of the world He will show us the way that we are to go.

Hope makes your spirit quiet in times of distress. Then you can hear God's voice telling you the way He needs you to go. Isa 43:31 assures us that, "Those who hope in the Lord will renew their strength. They will soar on wings as eagles; they will run and not grow weary, they will walk and not faint." This hope in the Lord is not a wishful thinking kind of hope but a certain trusting that becomes 'hope in action' expecting the Lord's result.

The effect that these five weapons have on Satan is to confuse, bewilder and frustrate him. God's enemy cannot understand God's ways. I'm sure you have all seen the clever advertisements for

'Nicorette Gum' with the little demon that tries to get the person to continue smoking but ends up being crushed by the gum package. Only his wriggling forked tail is left sticking out after the person has refused to give in to the smoking enticement. Our efforts to defeat Satan are a bit like that. That is not to say that we should underestimate his power and schemes. But the weapons of Jesus are extremely effective in defeating anything Satan can throw at us.

So how do these weapons apply to us as 'ezers'? One of our four tasks is to be a theologian and to bring the ways of God into every life experience. These five weapons–waiting, fellowship/relationship, covenant, purity and hope–are all based firmly in the word of God which 'ezers' are meant to bring forth in our position of half of the Blessed Alliance. It is the task of the 'ezer' to know God's word, teach God's word in her family and share God's word with her partner/husband and friends. It is symbolized at Shabbat on a Friday night by the mother of the family lighting the candles. Is it any wonder that women–'ezers'–are pressured by the world to not make waves, to be compliant and to live under shame, guilt and condemnation? A fully-armed 'ezer' is a real threat to the adversary–she is armed and dangerous! Hear God's voice calling each of us to rise up and declare the commands of the Lord.

Chapter 13
EXPLORING VALUE

In April, 2013 Paul and I went to New Zealand to celebrate our 50th wedding anniversary. It is Paul's birthplace and where many of his cousins still live. All his aunts and uncles have passed on–or as our Jewish friends say–now 'of blessed memory'! He had not been back for nearly 30 years and there were tremendous changes–not all of them good. I prayed in tongues a LOT when we were being driven anywhere as the roads are narrow and windy and everyone speeds along at 80 kph or more. They also drive on the wrong side of the road so it really felt extremely unsafe from where I sat! Homosexual marriage was approved by parliament while we were there and the country was suffering from a severe drought that had turned all the pasture land brown.

Church had been a large part of Paul's growing up years but it seemed that with the death of the previous generation the spiritual life of the country and the extended family had also died. One of the cousins that we stayed with for a week, challenged me one afternoon, when he said "Do you really believe all that stuff in the Bible?" I replied quite definitely that, indeed I do believe the Bible.

He then said "Do you really think that the whole vast, enormous universe could possibly have been created in just seven days?" "Yes I do." "You seem fairly intelligent but that doesn't make any sense at all. How could that possibly be true? And if I can't believe the first page of the Book why would I believe any of the rest of it?" "Well, how long is a day?" "Even if a day was 500 years long it would be impossible to create the entire universe in 3,500 years!"

I was shocked that his thinking was so limited. It has never occurred to him that a day on Earth might be 24 hours or so but a day on Jupiter or Mars, or even Pluto, might be different. And a day in this constellation has a certain time span but that does not necessarily apply to every constellation. When we use the word 'day' it can sometimes mean an indeterminate period of time not just 24 hours. I think we have all heard an older person use the expression "in my day...." and that definitely did not mean 24 hours! Because of what I considered a very small stumbling block, this cousin had closed his mind to any revelation of the Lord God who loves him. We came home resolved to pray with a lot more knowledge of how the cousins are thinking but also with a great many questions and ponderings in our minds. How can we reach someone, especially one we really care about, whose mind is so closed? How did Jesus reach people? How did the early church grow so explosively? What is making the church in China grow so astonishingly when they are subject to so much persecution and precious few resources? Where do we begin?

I didn't quite go back to Genesis but almost! The Lord reminded me of the verse in Psalm 103:7 where David says, "He (the Lord) made known his ways to Moses, his deeds to the people of Israel:" That is a very big key. It is God Himself who makes His ways known to a person or to a group of people. The first thing to realize is that the

Lord WANTS to be known. He is not hiding and He promises in Jer. 29:13 that if we seek him with all our hearts that He will be found. It is God who initiates this process and we can choose to accept His friendship overtures or not. We can determine whether we will seek out His ways or be content with watching His deeds. We can be active in this process and learn His ways or we can be observers and see only His deeds. When it says that God **made** His ways known to Moses we need to understand that it didn't happen all at once, nor at Moses' instigation. Over a period of time Moses and God developed a relationship with one another while Moses was tending sheep in the pasture lands near Mount Horeb. It is not that Moses didn't have a choice and was made to do something he really didn't want to do but that a relationship was built that enabled Moses to know God in a very special way by doing things with Him that revealed the Lord's thinking process and values. When Moses approached that burning bush it may not have been anything more than to satisfy his curiosity on his part. God was calling Moses for His own purposes. God had a big plan and chose Moses to be the one to lead His people out of Egypt but first Moses needed to learn to walk a different path than he had been walking before. A path will open that will lead us into more intimacy with the Lord if we choose to go that way. The Lord will not push Himself to be known by us until we are willing to come closer to Him.

We have a great tendency to look at our own failures and short-comings and dismiss the thought that the Lord God wants to be <u>**our**</u> friend, <u>**My**</u> friend. Moses initial response was to say to God that he was not really suitable because he couldn't talk very well. In effect Moses said "Here am I, Lord but please send my brother Aaron; he already lives in Egypt and he's a much better speaker than I am." To paraphrase, "Here am I Lord. Send Aaron"! We can become so focussed on ourselves that we fall easily into the role of a spectator instead of a participant. We are experts at discounting ourselves. And that is exactly where the enemy of our souls wants us to be!

Many years ago now my Dad, who was 85 at the time, was in extended care and suffering from the effects of strokes and mild dementia. I went to visit him one Sunday afternoon, very coincidentally just after a drama group had presented a play about the Prodigal Son. I found a quiet room where Dad and I could visit and I asked him what he would say to Jesus if Jesus was to walk into the room. Dad replied "Oh I don't think He would be bothered with the likes of me. He has more important things to do." I assured him that indeed Jesus would sit down with him and would want to have a good visit. I asked Dad if he had ever asked Jesus to come and live in his heart and, if not, would he like to? My Dad agreed and I had the privilege of leading him in a prayer inviting the Lord into his life. Then he said "I have waited all my life for somebody to pray that kind of prayer with me." That brought me to tears.

In our Western mindset we have a very individualistic attitude to life. A few years ago Frank Sinatra sang a song that so epitomizes that attitude–"I'll Do It My Way". Frank did do things his way but, though it brought lots of fame and money, it didn't seem to bring him much lasting pleasure or fulfillment. In John 15:16 Jesus makes the astounding statement that "You did not choose me but I chose you to go and bear fruit–fruit that will last." Like God's plan for Moses to lead the Israelites out of slavery in Egypt, the Father has a plan for us to lead people out of the bondage of sin in our day too. Also like Moses we must be taught God's ways, learn to have a relationship with Jesus and live the reality of Jesus being our Lord. Referring to

Jesus as Lord is not just a polite title. It includes an invitation to intimacy, a decision to be obedient to all His commands with a bond of love that will stretch into eternity.

As I have pondered what it means to know God's ways I think that the biggest lesson that Moses learned about God's ways is that God is Holy and that He calls us to also be holy through our relationship with Him. That doesn't mean that we will not sin but it does mean that we will be set apart for God's purposes, to enable us to truly call Him Lord, knowing that He loves us with an everlasting love. That calls for obedience, recognizing His voice and understanding the tasks that are set before us.

In Psalm 131–which is only 3 verses long–David addressed the whole situation of growing in our relationship with the Lord and declared that we need to be mature and become as weaned children, no longer demanding to be nursed and constantly cared for. There have been quite a number of times that I have grumbled about the Lord not hearing and answering my prayers the way I want and especially when I want. That is a very childish attitude (which I have since repented of–mostly!). I feel that I am gradually maturing as I learn to truly trust that God's ways are not my ways and His ways are always best. It is a process that doesn't happen all at once. It begins by having a realistic understanding of my own value and worth from God's point of view. Believe me, I know all my faults and it is much easier to look at all those things and see only reasons to discount myself from a relationship with our holy God. The one who is described as the "enemy of my soul" is always very ready and happy to remind me of every last fault and sometimes I think he even makes up a few! Too often I agree with him.

When I went to a Ladies Retreat one autumn, I saw an illustration of our value that was just brilliant. Our speaker was Heather Harmon from London, Ontario and she put it like this. She held up a $20.00 bank note and asked how much it was worth? Who set its value? If you add another $20.00 note with it does that change its value? It was such a simple illustration. Then she asked what is your value? Who set your value and what was that based on? You are made in God's image so how much are you worth? How much is God worth? Be assured that Satan will try to steal your worth unless you guard what the Lord has entrusted to you.

My thinking went one step further. The value and buying power of our Canadian $20.00 note stays at $20.00 so long as we stay in Canada. It doesn't matter if we use a brand new note or an older one made of different material. (Our newest bank notes in Canada are made of a very odd polymer substance that you can see through and makes them very difficult to counterfeit.) So age doesn't change the value. But if we cross the border and go to a different country–for example, the United States–the value of that note may well change because it was not made in that country. If we stay in God's kingdom our value remains constant according to the Maker's value system. But if we happen to wander into Satan's domain we can be certain that we will be devalued pretty quickly. We are still made in God's image but in Satan's realm he considers us to just be made of dirt!

Perhaps the place where we are most vulnerable is the whole issue of shame. There are things in our past that we all would give anything to erase and forget! It is a strange phenomenon that there are times when I have trouble remembering my phone number but I sure can remember those things that cause me shame!! Shame ruins us. Shame causes us to feel that we are worthless and fatally flawed and can never be counted as "good enough." We become victims of our circumstances, our history, and our own distorted self-worth. We look to others to tell us who we are and we compare ourselves in a weird spirit of competition that ensures that we always come out second (or third) best! It is that self-assigned worth that Satan loves to attack because it is based on the lie that Jesus can't possibly love a sinner as wicked as I am. In such a state it is impossible to receive compliments or positive feedback. It is also impossible to volunteer to serve as a warrior in the Lord's army that is needed to build His kingdom.

So we do one of two things. Either we hide like Adam and Eve did and deny and accuse one another. Or we build a false, fantasy identity that tries to bluff our way through life. It can be unrealistically brilliant or overly humble, but it is not based in the truth of who we actually are. It doesn't matter to Satan just so long as it is based on a lie and not truth. But the net result is that we are unable to enjoy a totally open, intimate relationship with other people and most of all with God. Intimacy is not based on works but on open, trusting relationships–simply doing things together–and we must remove all those blocks that prevent us from knowing and being known by our most loving God. Included in those activities that grow relationship are playing games (ever played a game with Jesus? I guarantee you will be surprised!), watching a sunrise or sunset together, just sitting quietly with a cup of tea–or coffee, learning what Jesus' love language is and sharing Him with other people. The possibilities are endless.

When we begin to break down our self-imposed barricades to the Father's love we can begin to grow in our identity and embrace our destiny. We can seek the Father's forgiveness with true humility and trust that He will never abandon us. It really is rather foolish to try to hide what we've done–or not done–from the One who knows all things, sees all things and will pursue us until He catches us. In this life there are innumerable opportunities for misunderstandings, offences, hurts, resentments, rebellion, frenzied activity and a host of other activities to make us stumble in our search for identity that leads to destiny. It begins with our relationship with our earthly father.

When Ed Piorek was in Victoria in May 2013, he said that "the father wound is so deep, and all pervasive, that its healing could well be the most radical social reform conceivable." Fatherhood has always been under attack but never more so than in the last 100 years or so. At the beginning of the 20th century everything was gearing up for the most massive war that the earth had ever seen. Men from all over the world gathered in Europe to fight and kill one another with the most horrendous weapons ever invented. On the land, the sea and even from the air death and disease destroyed homes, cities, farm lands, hopes, dreams and love. For the most part it was men who were on the front lines in that war. Men who were fathers and potential fathers would eventually return to their homes as broken, disillusioned, desperately hurt creatures–if they returned at all. A great many of those men–including my grandfather–would never speak of what they had experienced. For far too many of them any faith they had in God was killed along with the soldiers they had shot at for four years. Their spirits were irrevocably broken.

About 20 years later the whole world went to war a second time. By this time the machines of war were more powerful, the technology was vastly improved and it was not just men fighting in this new outbreak but women as well, both civilians and in the military. This time it took six years before an Allied victory was declared. The bullets killed millions; starvation and disease killed more millions and despair drained hope from many millions more. The 20th century was not quite 50 years old at that point, but already two generations of fathers had been decimated! Before the century was another 50 years older there were at least two more wars that took men and women away from their homes, farms and occupations, in order to fight against the tyrannies of evil that never give up. The scars that have been left behind are not so obvious on the surface anymore but the wounds that caused those scars remain, are very deep and are festering just below the surface. I believe there is a direct line between those wounds and the rampant alcoholism, drug addiction, divorce, violence, disobedience and rebellion in children and youth, and widespread disillusionment and hopelessness that is afflicting our present society.

As the hellish fires of war were cooling all over the world there was a growing discontent in the Christian church especially in Europe and North America. People were questioning their faith which didn't seem to have been strong enough to withstand all the grief and sorrow that are an inevitable part of war. Where had God been? Why had He not prevented all that suffering? Were all the stories learned in Sunday School just that–just stories? Did anything good at all come out of all those years of destruction? Are we really meant to believe the verse in Romans 8:28 that says that "all things work together for good for those who love God and are called according to His purposes?" Does anybody really believe <u>that</u> in the face of all the destruction? Gradually church buildings were closed, or sold, or turned into museums or restaurants. Though we didn't recognise it then, and perhaps still don't now, the Lord was getting ready to breathe new life into His body here on earth to bring forth a new reformation.

We have to take a much longer view of history than a mere 50–70 years in order to see what God was up to during those years. For too many people the Christian faith was simply a formality. It was a familiar, comforting, routine religion that had very little power or authority left in it. This is exactly the attitude that Paul's cousin in New Zealand is living with. There was no expectation of miracles that could be counted on, if Jesus was in very truth LORD of your life and not just a character in a storybook. It was not that people were necessarily leaving God out of their lives but they didn't know that He wanted to be **in** their everyday lives. They were consumed with mortgages, vehicle insurance, babies, and what to cook for dinner. People had lost touch with their Maker.

They also stopped believing their Bibles. I read a statistic recently that claimed that in North America less that 3% of people who claim to be Christians read their Bibles every day and a further 10% read it less than once a month. The other 87% didn't bother to read the Book at all. I found in one of my journals an entry dated Feb 27, 2011. What I had written was this: "I heard the Lord say to me as I was waking up this morning; "God is not a theory. He is not a philosophy. God is not a good idea or a 'force'. God is a Person. He is a Person you can have a relationship with. Your Bible is not a text book. It is not a 'Do It Yourself Book' or a 'Self Help Book'. Your Bible is not a poetry book or a recipe book. Your Bible is a Book you must LIVE!" One way of looking at it is that it is the Owners Manual full of instructions and safety warnings. We run into serious trouble when we neglect to read the whole book, including the history, the Prophets and all the writings of the Psalms and Proverbs. There is no other book that we read at any time that we just choose a verse here, a paragraph there, and a chapter somewhere else and expect to have the whole story.

Out of the ashes and devastation of the 20th century several things can be seen to be in the process of emerging. In WWI, the Lord removed the strangle hold the Turkish Ottoman Empire had on the lands of the Middle East. The political earthquake that resulted re-aligned most of the nations of that area and created whole new economic dynamics based on oil that are still being worked out today. Then in WWII, the Lord drastically shook the whole world after the holocaust of the Jewish people and paved the way for the establishment of the new state of Israel.

The Lord also drastically shook the complacent establishment that controlled the church and introduced her once again to the Holy Spirit! The spiritual revolution that began with the Pentecostal movement around the beginning of the 20th century had introduced, by the time we reached the 1970's, a new noisy, charismatic movement was causing chaos in many corners of the church. Some people saw only division in the church as a result, but others saw a fresh wind blowing away the dust and cobwebs. I believe that if we can try to look at things from God's point of view, Jesus is retrieving His Bride, His church, and as He did to Moses so long ago, is now making His ways known to us. He is teaching us what it really means for Jesus to be LORD!!

Just as we have to tear down derelict buildings in order to build something new so the Lord has had to 'tear down', or allow to die, parts of the church that were no longer staying true to HIS ways. We need to identify those ways so that we stay attuned to what the Lord is wanting to do. I suspect that we are living in a new construction zone in the church and perhaps we should put up signs that say "Hard Hats Advisable! Construction Zone!" We need to get back to knowing what God's ways are and refuse to compromise with what just feels good because this is the way we have always done it before. Jesus wants a new Kingdom built on love, joy, peace, patience, kindness, goodness, gentleness, faithfulness and self control. The challenge is enormous. But we have a sure promise from Jesus, Himself, that He is the master builder "and the gates of Hades shall not overpower it." Matt 16: 18 (NASB)

Chapter 14

LAMBS, DOGS AND THE FUTURE REMATCH

One afternoon I laid down hoping to have a short nap. That seemed to be a signal to the Lord that it was a good time for a chat instead. I finally had to get up and find my Bible to really understand what He was saying to me. Over and over I kept hearing "the Bride made herself ready". How does a bride make herself ready, I wondered, and who is this 'bride' exactly?

Jesus started the conversation by reminding me of a time when Paul and I lived in New Zealand and had gone to visit our friends Jack and Gladys McKenzie who had a sheep farm in the south of the country. It was a lovely autumn weekend, cool enough to want a jacket but brilliantly sunny and bright. Jack invited us to go with him to move some lambs from one paddock to another. He took five dogs with us and we climbed into the farm truck for a short drive across green rolling farmland. Four of the dogs were very experienced but one was relatively new and was paired with an older veteran. Jack explained that lambs are very hard to work with because they don't know what they are supposed to do. Lambs and dogs have to learn how to work together.

When Jack stopped the truck and opened the gate the dogs poured off the back and were soon racing around the perimeter of the field. Using only whistles and shouts he directed the dogs to round up and move nearly 200 lambs to where he wanted them to go. It was amazing to watch! The dogs were positioned around the edges of the flock and gradually moved them into a smaller flock towards the centre of the field. But the lambs were not sure which way to run and the dogs were constantly dashing around to prevent escape in the wrong direction. A couple of times the racing white stream came close to where the open gate was but the lambs spooked and had to be redirected by the dogs. Eventually a river of woolly white bodies spilled through the gate and spread out to where fresh green pasture waited for them. The panting dogs flopped to the ground with tongues hanging out and Jack lavished them with praise for a job well done!

The point the Lord was trying to get me to understand was that dogs and lambs had to learn how to work together to do what the master shepherd needed. In the same way men and women also have to learn to understand the Shepherd's whistles and directions to get His job done! At this time we do not seem to be very good at doing that. We are too concerned with control, competition and individual ambition to be able to appreciate the development of co-operatively building God's kingdom "on earth as it is in heaven". Without having a very clear idea of what goes on in heaven we seem to be totally focussed on how to perfect our earth so it could feel like heaven without having to change our attitudes and activities. I feel we have tried to miniaturize God so He can fit into our wants and plans in 'our' world.

The Lord then started to bring scriptures to my mind. In Genesis 3:8 it says that "the man and his wife heard the sound of the Lord God as he was walking in the garden in the cool of the day". I wonder how many times the three of them walked together in the garden before the serpent showed up? What did they talk about? I am certain that the Lord God would have warned them about the serpent since He had already warned them about the tree they were not to eat from.

I read in a Jewish commentary that before the Fall Adam did not need to use any tools to tend the Garden of God but just needed to speak to His creation to bring forth new growth or pruning. Sounds like what Jesus did to the fig tree in Matt 21:19. He also spoke to the storm on the Sea of Galilee and it stopped. Jesus told His disciples in Matt 17:20 that faith the size of a mustard seed would enable them to speak to a mountain and it would move. To most of us moving mountains would need much more faith than a mere mustard seed, surely! In an earlier chapter I shared how we spoke to the mountain of our indebtedness and it was removed, much to our amazement! In Matt 8: 1-4 Jesus cleansed a man of leprosy with just a word of command. In the same chapter, a Roman centurion asked for healing for his servant and Jesus was astonished when the man declared that all it takes is a word from Jesus and it will be so. Jesus raised Jairus' daughter and His friend Lazarus from the dead with just a spoken word as well. In the Old Testament Moses was told to 'speak' to the rock to get water to flow, but he struck the rock instead and lost his place for going into the Promised Land. I believe that it was not just a case of disobedience but was much more than that. Father God was inviting Moses into a level of intimacy and authority on an even higher level than that which Moses had already enjoyed, getting closer to what Adam had been privileged to have. But Moses failed the test.

There are not many words recorded before the Fall and those few that are spoken are very affirming words. However, immediately following the Satanic deception, the words from Adam and Eve towards each other reflect the poison that was in the fruit of the forbidden tree. Previously, words were used to make things grow but after eating the poison, words brought shame, blame, guilt and avoidance between God and the first couple and each other. It was the beginning of a long destructive pattern of using words to hurt, and destroy relationships that continues to this very day.

In spite of warnings in every book of our Bibles, most of us are not very careful with our words. In Matt 12:36 Jesus said, "But I tell you that men will have to give an account on the day of judgement for every careless word they have spoken". That word 'men' includes women! How different relationships would be if we gave more thought before we speak.

I am becoming more and more convinced that preparations are well under way for the rematch between Satan and the daughters of Eve and sons of Adam that was promised in Gen 3:15. The Lord God said to the serpent, "And I will put enmity between you and the woman, and between your offspring and hers; he will crush your head, and you will strike his heel". The word enmity means so much more than simple hatred. It is implacable, irresolvable, totally destructive hatred of an enemy–a fight to the death! The battle that was lost in the Garden of Eden will not be lost a second time.

Unfortunately the poisonous words exchanged between the first couple has continued ever since that disastrous day, to divide men and women from God's original purpose of co-operation and mutual support of each other in tending His Garden. The effects of war, violence, sexual exploitation, poverty and every other social problem proves again and again that Satan continues to inspire harm to God's beloved children. Bitter, angry words are his favourite weapon! But change is coming! And it is women who must be in the forefront to begin that change process. It was to women that the risen Messiah first appeared, women were the first to touch Him and it was women who were first told to "Go and tell" that Jesus is alive!

If we go back to the original picture that the words 'ezer knegdo' illustrate, of the river with two banks and the river of life flowing between them, we easily see that the tasks of men and women are not identical but equally necessary. Women were to identify the enemy, identify his tactics, develop a strategy to defeat those tactics and then work with men to put the strategy into place. In the process she will establish boundaries–spiritual boundaries–that will first of all protect her children and the men in her community, and especially her husband if she is married. For too many years Satan succeeded in intimidating women into thinking that they are not able, or worthy, or equipped to be spiritual leaders. Like Eve, women have believed a lie. Satan has smothered women with shame, guilt, fear and isolation and at the same time deceived men with anger, violence and distrust. God's original intention for men and women to work together for mutual support was largely defeated before it had even started. That is a huge generality of course. Before there can be a rematch that situation must change.

When we take a viewpoint that is bigger than just looking at our own denomination, or religion, or nation, a very gradual change has been taking place in this world that God considers His own! He made **ALL** people not just Christians and Jews and He has not stopped being concerned about them just because they have a different view of Him. Coming straight from God's throne is an overwhelming assurance that God loves His sons and daughters with an everlasting love! Paul's letter to Titus says in chapter 2:11, "For the grace of God has appeared bringing salvation to all men". That word 'all' includes Buddhists, agnostics, Islamists, beggars, murderers, prostitutes, orphans and university professors to name just a few! The invitation to salvation is universal but it requires individuals to put their faith in Jesus inviting Him to be Lord of their lives. As preparations were being made to welcome the 21st century, millions of Christians around the world prayed intensely for the peoples of the "10/40 Window"–that area of the earth from 10 degrees N to 40 degrees N where most of the unreached peoples live. Spiritual and social revolution has characterized those countries in the following years but there has also been much determined preaching of the Gospel.

There is a move all over the world to bring changes, especially for women! Girls are being taught to read, and write and it is dramatically changing their lives. Educated women bring change to government, standards of living and the preparation of the next generation. This can sometimes be a violent struggle as the world saw when a young girl in Pakistan was shot on a school bus just because she wanted an education. That young girl was Malala Yusefsai who has since been granted a Nobel Peace Prize and become a great champion for women's education everywhere. Poverty-stricken women in Asia and Africa are receiving micro loans and being taught business practices that enable them to provide for their families and send their children to school. The poverty cycle is being broken by ministering to the needs they have right now. For example, a young, 15 year old prostitute in Kampala, Uganda, was asked why she was not afraid of contracting Aids. Her reply was heart breaking! She said, "Aids is two years down the road; I need food today!" It is not enough to bring her out of prostitution. She must be enabled to earn an income from a legitimate job that builds her self esteem rather than degrades who she was created to be. In Africa, where the terrible Aids epidemic has destroyed so many families, it is the grandmothers who are left to raise the grandchildren. Help is coming to those women from co-operatives of grandmothers in North American cities who raise funds and take other practical help to the African grandmothers. Women must help women!

God paints with a very large brush! When I first read Psalm 68:12 I realized that when it said "she that remains at home will divide the spoils" it was talking about women who live peaceful Christian lives needing to faithfully pray and support women in other parts of the world who don't enjoy such freedom. This became an absolute conviction after I attended the Knesset Christian Allies Conference in Jerusalem in 2007 as I outlined in chapter 6. The theme for that Conference was "I am my Sister's Keeper" and was based on Ps 68:11–the verse that under-girds this book. We need to expand our understanding of the extent of the love in God's heart for all women everywhere and pray for them knowing that our Almighty God knows the name of every last one of them! He does not *begin* to love them *after* they come to faith in His Son. They can only love the Son because *they are first loved by Father God*! This love-based relationship is totally dependent, from the start, on God's enormous, forgiving love.

Recently I came across a quote from Bill Johnson who is the pastor of Bethel church in Redding California. He said; "When you avoid a battle you were born for, you face a battle you are not equipped for." For millennia we have been facing an ugly battle with Satan that we have tried to fight on his terms, allowing his agenda.

But the battle we were born for is still in front of us. Rev 19:7-8 declares that "The marriage supper of the Lamb has come and the bride has <u>made</u> herself ready; fine linen has been given to her to wear." The bride that is being talked about consists of both men and women of faith. For the bride to be 'ready' she must have finally worked out how to enable men and women to co-operatively battle together to defeat Satan. Our individualistic Western mindset must bow before the pressing needs to build community and cooperation for the sake of the Kingdom of God. Only the Holy Spirit is able to 'give' the bride the clean linen garments that she will need to wear for this battle. Verse 8 concludes by saying that "Fine linen stands for the righteous acts of the saints".

"The Lord gives the command; the women who proclaim the good news are a great host."(NASB) We have very exciting days ahead of us. Are we listening for that command? If we know whose daughter we are, we will truly be able to invite whomever we meet into our Father's house. Even so, Come Lord Jesus!

CPSIA information can be obtained at www.ICGtesting.com
Printed in the USA
LVOW07s0359080815

449314LV00001B/19/P